11/11/2013

Wash DC

SOULS UNDER SIEGE

I've been blessed to be immersed with thousands of young men and women in uniform and to know firsthand their issues. I also know the truth and fortitude with which they keep moving forward. I am honored and privileged to be a witness on this journey.

—B. Cantrell, 2008

SOULS UNDER SIEGE

THE EFFECTS OF MULTIPLE TROOP DEPLOYMENTS AND HOW TO WEATHER THE STORM

Bridget C. Cantrell, Ph.D.

Souls Under Siege: The Effects of Multiple Troop Deployments—and How to Weather the Storm
Copyright © 2009 Bridget C. Cantrell, Ph.D.

Published by Hearts Toward Home International
    (an IRS Approved 501(c)(3) Public Charity)
1050 Larrabee Avenue
Suite 104, PMB 714
Bellingham, Washington 98225-7367

Graphic design by Suzanne Steel, Hot Steel Design,
www.hotsteeldesign.com
Edited by Shalene Takara and Christy Phillippe
Typeset and Interior Design by Rhiannon Jackson

Printed in the United States of America

DEDICATION

In honor of my late father, WWII and Korean combat veteran
Charlie Smith Cantrell
November 19, 1925 – March 9, 2008
and all other fallen warriors and their loved ones.

Acknowledgements

I would like to acknowledge and thank US Army Chaplain Steven Cantrell for all his support and encouragement of my work over the years, and to Chuck Dean for sharing his experiences and insights from a veteran's perspective so that my writing can always be made clear to those I want to touch. I deeply want to thank the men and women in uniform who have allowed me inside their lives so I can convey their thoughts with other warriors, their families, and community members across our country. Thanks to all those in my care and to my veteran friends and mentors, who have so graciously supported my endeavors to work with the current troops by keeping the home fires burning. It has been their way of contributing to the healing of our warriors who currently serve our country with honor and distinction. To Kalli, my assistant, for her support, and to my close friends, Dee (my inspiration) and Sandi, who have mentored me and shared my passion of caring for our most precious national treasure. Last but not least, to my mother, Carmen, my daughter, Alayna, and my brother, Charlie Bill, who have all shared *me* unconditionally with those I love and admire: our troops that sacrifice so much for us to live free. Thank you all from the bottom of my heart.

Contents

A Special Message to the Military

As with any book written for a military audience, proper honor and respect for your service is of paramount importance. Because our intention was to keep this work an easy read and to the point, I chose to use some general terms in identifying particular units and branches of service. I know the importance of maintaining unit recognition and esprit de corps and hope you understand that for the sake of content flow and simplicity, I have not delineated between Army, Navy, Air Force, Marine Corps, Coast Guard, National Guard, or Enlisted Reserve. I have attempted to simply use the term *troops* to identify every person for their service and sacrifice. I wanted to take this opportunity to brief you on this in advance in case I have inadvertently identified you all as only "soldiers." For this, I apologize. Thank you for your understanding.

> Most of the concepts in my books can easily crossover from strictly military experiences to (1) anyone whose work requires extended separations from home and/or loved ones, and (2) those who have chosen high risk, high stress occupations. For example, private contractors working in war zones can certainly benefit from the information I have compiled here. Currently, the US has troops deployed and private contractors working for the Defense Department around the globe. This has placed a tremendous burden upon the individuals involved (including the loved ones at home). It is my wish that what I have written here can be used in a universal way.

Combat Operational Stress (COS)
and Post-Traumatic Stress Disorder (PTSD)

To date, perhaps more than a million US troops have served in Iraq since the invasion, and tens of thousands have shown signs of serious stress upon their return. Throughout this book, you will not only read about some of these stress reactions, but you will also learn how to deal with and recognize many of the symptoms as they arise. War fighters may or may not return home with what is diagnosed as "post-traumatic stress disorder" (PTSD). Many of the signs of PTSD may be mistaken for what is now termed by military stress teams as Combat Operational Stress (COS). It has been determined that every participant in a war zone *will* manifest some symptoms of COS (i.e. hyper-alertness, anxiety, frustration, anger, confusion, intolerance of "stupid behavior", sleep disruption, etc.), but this does not indicate that the person has PTSD. However, readjustment issues are common and to be expected. If they continue to worsen or interfere with the quality of your relationships or with your life in general, then take the steps to find help. It is my intent that as you read this book, you will be able to

INTRODUCTION

The Seige

The Battle of Khe Sanh, conducted in northwestern Quang Tri Province, Republic of Vietnam, between January 21 and April 8, 1968, brought the reality of a *siege* into modern times.

For the sake of history, at Khe Sanh the combatants were comprised of elements of the United States III Marine Amphibious Force, elements of the South Vietnamese Army of the Republic of Vietnam, and two or three division-sized elements of the People's Army of Vietnam. During a seventy-seven-day period, Khe Sanh Combat Base and the hilltop outposts around it were under constant North Vietnamese ground and artillery attacks. The Marines were literally cut off, and for those seventy-seven days, innovative methods had to be used to keep the warriors supplied with the means to live and continue the fight.

So what is a siege and how does it pertain to this writing? A siege is a time-honored military maneuver that armies have deployed since ancient times. It is a strategy used to surround and hopefully conquer objectives by using time and attrition to wear down and overwhelm those who are besieged.

On the other hand, those who are under siege may be safe and hold their ground as long as they have prepared well enough in advance for such adversity and danger.

I believe the idea of a "siege" can also portray the circumstances in which many of our present military personnel find themselves as they face multiple deployments. The real enemy is not the government or military commands or even the hostile forces they must encounter while down range. The most voracious enemy of all for our troops and families is time, attrition, and unpreparedness. Those are the elements that continue to eat away at every level of the lives of our warriors and their loved ones. Those under siege must find ways to hold their ground as long as this war lasts, and they need to prepare well in advance for the inevitability of multiple deployments.

Evan Kanter, MD, Ph.D., staff psychiatrist in the PTSD Outpatient Clinic of the VA Puget Sound Health Care System, states that one major risk factor for PTSD, or post-traumatic stress disorder, is the unprecedented multiple deployments to a combat zone (Kanter, 2006). For the troops, time and the wearing away of attrition is a formidable enemy. It has been shown that those on their second, third and fourth tours of duty have sharply greater rates of mental health challenges than those on their first deployments. In reality, what this means is that there may be increasing issues with such PTSD symptoms as sleep disturbance, startle response, anger issues, irritability, excess alcohol, drug use, etc.

For the families, the primary enemy is not being prepared for such emotional changes and upheavals that may come about as a result of the revolving door of deployments.

In this present war, many people are looking for a quick fix to win it, fight it, or end it. In the meantime, some worn-out men and women are burdened with another concern: the window of seemingly endless combat tours.

Presently, I am regularly embedded with thousands of troops who have returned from the war. My job as a therapist, teacher, lecturer and now, a friend, is to equip them with effective tools to make healthy transitions from the combat zone to a world of peace. However, because of the likelihood of another tour on the horizon, for most of them the transitioning information I offer is highly transitory. Although my workshops and counseling sessions are appreciated and of high value to the returning troops, each time is laced below the surface with lingering thoughts of having to return to the war in the near future. I do know that the idea of redeployment, that is looming over the heads of our military community, presents challenges for them to get treatment until the war comes to an end. These multiple deployments, along with lengthy fifteen-month tours, wreak ongoing havoc on the psyches and relationships of our volunteer military. The effects on our society as a whole in the future are still unknown, but society, too, will surely be heavily impacted for years to come.

This is the siege of the soul, and, as a therapist, finding ways to help support and send "supplies" into these besieged areas has become a responsibility that I accept with all my heart. As with any work in my profession, the effort will have been more than worth it if I can impart just one positive tool—one anchoring thought—and if one life can be changed for the better. The thrust of this book is not only to expand awareness of the issues involved, but also to outline some sensible tools for finding relief in these trying times. My suggestions are the result of many hands-on observations, and countless hours of interfacing with our military personnel, their leaders, and family members.

It is my hope that every war fighter and/or family member who reads this book will have a better life as a result. I do what I do in an effort to inform, educate and help those who must bear the burden of going off to war to pick up the pieces in their lives . Hopefully what I offer here will help in some way to achieve that objective.

With My Deepest Respect and Gratitude,
Bridget C. Cantrell, Ph.D.

PART ONE

CHAPTER ONE

The Revolving Door

But she had heard the songs and the slogans and seen the parades, had been to the meetings, and though it was her son leaving she did not think it would be so bad. Nobody thought it would be so bad. Nobody thought it could be so bad. And all the officers and politicians and newspapers said it would be a month or two, no longer....
                                    – Gary Paulsen, *Soldier's Heart*

"Hey guys, I'm your good-luck charm. If I'm out with ya, things'll be okay." The young sergeant on his third tour in Iraq bolstered his squad's morale before they began the day's patrol. He reminded them that since he had made it through his eighth month on this tour, he must be impervious to danger. However, inside...deep in his soul...his underlying concern was much more than he wanted to let on. Saying things like this had become part of his routine to convince himself that he and his troops would make it safely through another day in the "sandbox."

It was close to noon when the squad ran into a small group of children. As usual, they stopped to mess around with them and proceeded to stuff candy into their outstretched hands. As quick and unexpected as things can happen on any street in Iraq, a fleeting shadow approached, and it was the last thing the young battle-hardened sergeant, three of his men, and several children would see of this life. A suicide bomber struck hard and fast.

Incidents like this can happen on any tour of duty—first, second, third, or any thereafter. I begin this book not to tell another war story, and I do not write it to necessarily point out the very real horrors of a war that is currently being waged. The above incident, as sad as it is, primarily is an illustration to portray just one of the many thousands of soul-impacting aspects of war. It is a very real and heart-wrenching example of troops at war, but what is not written here is the agony that those families and friends of the casualties must endure for all the years to follow. It is heart-wrenching to see the Gold Star Parents stand up in a room to be honored and loved.

A friend, a Vietnam veteran, once told me that dying is never for the dead—it is always for the living, and the intense ground-level stress that today's warriors face with multiple deployments is only half of the story. While many of us go about the business of working to reduce the emotional and psychological fallout on the engaged troops, we also run head-on into a maze of frustrations, inner conflicts, and the challenges of family members and friends at home who are trying to cope with their loved one's presence in the war zone. I personally know many parents whose children have been lost in the line of duty or have been severely impacted by a war-zone trauma. Some of these parents have taken their pain and put it into action to help other parents or family members in order to make a difference. It is their way of saying that their loved one's sacrifice was not in vain.

Shifting Expectations and Reality

I do not wish to make this a book of doom and gloom, but rather one that educates and gives hope for all those involved. So, in the midst of all the possible negative implications connected to multiple deployments, I have found that many family members are finding a positive side to the separations.

The first that comes to mind is that after the first deployment, subsequent tours of duty do not hit the family in such a mysterious way. Many of the unknowns of the initial deployment no longer exist. The families, including their loved one down range, have survived one tour, and there is some relief in knowing more about what to expect the next time around. Even though each deployment is different, there are some stages that remain familiar.

During the first deployment, the news may become a steady diet, and sometimes disturbing reports are broadcast about situations and events taking place where their loved one is stationed. The fear that envelops those at home goes without saying. However, when the service member comes home and the families are given information about the actual duties they performed, the mystique of a second deployment is lessened. They realize that many of the circumstances they saw on TV were not necessarily the entire picture of what goes on in the war zone. It is comforting for them to learn that Iraq and Afghanistan are big countries and that many dangers broadcast by the media about certain hot spots had very little to do with their loved one. Like the old saying goes, "The truth shall set you free," and as families discover more about their loved one's actual duties in the war zone, they acquire a new awareness and a greater sense of emotional freedom. On subsequent tours, expectations can shift dramatically and the family then becomes a "veteran" and "survivor" in their own right.

Just having an awareness of what to expect does wonders in reducing excess worry. It is very important for your warrior to return home to a place where stress is reduced and expectations are realistic and comfortable. This type of predictable routine and calm environment serves to reduce or eliminate undue distress for all on the home front.

A Revolving Door Built for Two

Military couples experience challenges that many civilians do not. Multiple long-term separations can create harmful effects upon even the best of relationships. When I wrote the workbook course *Once a Warrior: Wired for Life, An Interactive Workbook* (previously titled *Turning Your Heart Toward Home*), it was designed for couples, not individuals, to assess their preparedness for reuniting *together* upon returning from a war zone. It has since helped many couples and individuals survive the challenges posed by military life, including multiple deployments. As a review, we will take a look at some of the teachings of that course later in this book.

A massive number of service men and women in uniform are already on their third and fourth deployment to war-torn countries like Iraq and Afghanistan. During such separations, most warriors, couples, and family members have discovered a variety of ways to communicate. E-mail, instant messages, video conferencing, and cell phones have all taken the twenty-first-century warrior into a new digital world of rapid connection with those at home. As in all previous wars, having a source of communication with home keeps the connection alive and strong. For the service person engaged in war situations, communication provides an incredible source of hope. What partners at home must become aware of, and accept, is the fact that connecting is sometimes impossible…no matter what means of communicating is used. You must realize that operational circumstances may develop that may prevent you from linking, and there can be long periods with no communication at all.

Couples dealing with the realities and hardships of multiple deployments need to share their expectations about being apart from one another, as well as their expectations for once they are together again. As I have outlined in *Once a Warrior: Wired for Life, An Interactive Workbook*, the reunion stage requires greater sensitivity on the part of both the deployed service member as well as all members of his or her family. Reconnecting also may require some time alone and apart from children, parents, in-laws, and friends. This is something to consciously prepare for when working on making a healthy transition after each deployment. This is most certainly a community responsibility.

Expect, Prepare, Grow

Learn what to expect with each deployment—there is no need for surprises or psychological "ambushes."

Learn how to prepare for each deployment…they will not all be the same.

Recognize and acknowledge the positive growth in you, your partner, and your entire family because of this experience.

CHAPTER TWO

You're Going Where?

"I know it ain't right," she wrote in one letter,
"but you must think on coming home now."
— Gary Paulsen, *Soldier's Heart*

"We're extended!" The news spread rapidly through-out the brigade. Every soldier in the unit scrambled to find ways to text, call, instant message, or e-mail their loved ones in the States to break the bad news. They were not coming home as everyone had planned.

The situation in Baghdad had developed quickly and needed to be responded to without delay. The commanders in the field chose this particular brigade to stay and con-tinue operations because they were the most experienced team in the sandbox. Their work in Mosul had been out-standing and that success was their drawing card to be the most likely team to get the job done now.

The soldiers knew they must carry on and do what they were called upon to do, but those on the home front might not be as enthusiastic or understanding of the extension. It is difficult for loved ones and family to understand their warrior's desire to return down range. For some, it is the most important thing they have ever done in their lives; there is a great sense of honor, commitment and camaraderie that can hold an extremely powerful allure for our men and women in uniform. Those who are affected by these situations must make the best of these demands and keep moving forward. Honoring each other for their contributions is important in nourishing these relationships.

Extending tours of duty are part of any war. It is something the military tries to avoid, but most of the time it cannot be prevented. Extensions for warriors engaged in war zones, many times without any advanced notice, are inevitable. It makes little difference what war, what branch, or who is in charge of decision making whenever there is a prolonged conflict—it simply happens.

This sudden change throws off many plans, not just for the soldiers and their families, but in many different areas, including logistics, personnel and training. However, for the purposes of this book, my interest lies in how it affects our men and women in uniform and their families.

Initially, army soldiers were supposed to be on the ground in Iraq for a year, with two years of rest and recuperation between deployments. However, the length and intensity of the war has meant that these objectives have often been missed. In April 2007, the head of the US Joint Forces Command publicly announced that some soldiers might have to serve as long as sixteen months at a time, while others might have less than a year between rotations. This has become a reality of the current war.

From the numerous workshops I conduct and clinical hours I spend with active duty military and reservists from all branches of service, I have seen stigmas that are alive and well and that clearly interfere with our servicemen and women getting the much needed help they deserve. According to Hoge (2005), sixty-five percent of service members that were interviewed said that they would be perceived as weak by their unit members if they admitted to needing help (Hoge, 2005). So their concerns are mostly centered on how they would be seen by their comrades and leaders, and how it might affect not only their military careers, but their civilian careers as well. I personally know of many military leaders and chaplains who are working feverishly to change this attitude and dispel these stigmas by educating leaders to the importance of good mental health practices, not only for themselves, but for the men and women they serve both on and off the battlefield. This is tremendously important and a positive step forward. In order for healing to take place and be maintained, it is vital that open discussions about the events in one's life be fully explored. Linking the past with present behaviors, both adaptive and maladaptive, along with a person's experiences in the military, can provide a new understanding for the warrior. It also serves to build empathy and compassion within the entire support system or community.

Many years ago, while doing my research and writing to attain a doctorate in clinical psychology, I examined the effects of social support on the Vietnam veterans. I found that a strong and supportive social support network is a significant factor that contributes to a better level of functioning and adjustment. There are a variety of factors that serve to exacerbate combat weariness and that likely result in worsening the stress reactions to war. I also found that emotion-focused coping involving the rethinking of a situation is important in quieting down anxiety before moving into problem-focused coping. Problem-focused coping directly leads to active problem solving and making decisions based on realistic expectations. The journey home requires that a person create meaning and purpose for his or her life. This leads to better social relationships for the person and with the community to which he or she will return.

During the Vietnam War, army troops were only required to serve one tour that generally lasted one year. This varied according to the branch of service, but many of my patients from that war served more than their one-year tours. Some had reenlisted with the intention of making a career out of the military, while others simply had time enough left on their present enlistment to do a second tour. At the time, there was a sixty-day rule, which meant that after your return from the war zone in Southeast Asia, you were required to remain in a noncombat area of assignment for at least sixty days. Upon expiration of that limitation, you could be ordered back to another tour of duty. For the career-minded, upon reenlistment, a soldier virtually contracted to go back and forth to *any* combat zone as often as the government needed him and wanted to send him.

So, are there any redeeming factors to an extended tour in a war zone? A career Marine recently pointed out the benefits of his extended deployments. He mentioned that even though he was only a lance corporal, staying longer in the war zone gave him priority for future assignments. By willfully extending his duty time in Afghanistan, his chances for reassignment to less dangerous areas, such as Latin America or the Pacific, will be improved. He has been told that troops in Iraq and Afghanistan get first pick at slots in better and more exotic locations. So this is very attractive and enticing to a young warrior thinking of the future.

In addition to the attraction of a better duty assignment, if one hangs in longer, the custom is for the reenlisting troop to receive a host of tax-free financial incentives, including hazardous-duty pay, imminent-danger pay, and special-duty pay. However, many times unexpected extensions in a combat zone are due to logistical priorities (i.e., refurbishing or cleaning gear and weapons for the replacement unit to use when they arrive). However, when the planning goes awry, which it is known to do in large governmental services such as the armed forces, the length of a deployment can be longer than expected, at which time incentives also become nebulous.

Pseudo Short-Timer's Syndrome

During the Vietnam War, a one-year tour of duty compelled the troops to develop distinctive nomenclature as they spent time in the war zone. A *short-timer* was a person who was counting down to the very second when he would end his tour of duty and step on a plane or ship to come home. Since many arrived individually (not as part of a deployed unit), every service person had a particular date that they would *DEROS* (date of expected return from overseas) home. The less time one had left to go in-country, the more significant it became to be known as a *short-timer*. In 'Nam, this countdown became an important part of each warrior's process, and it usually called for immense cause for celebration along the way.

Short-timers, for the most part, became more demonstrative as the length of time they were to serve became shorter. In the array of daily celebrations, they developed a sense of elitism and a swaggering bravado due to the fact that their time was drawing to a close and they would soon leave the misery of war behind.

It was not uncommon for short-timers to daily set about reminding everyone within earshot that they would soon return to the United States. They had served their time, so many rituals, icons and exaggerated ceremonies were devised to remind everyone around them that their soon-to-be exit was no minor issue.

Calendars were drawn on flak jackets, hash marks on helmets, and notches carved on sticks. Since each troop had to endure months of having the short-timer business rubbed in his face, when their turn to be "short" came, they, too, went all out to exercise their rite of passage. As the war went on, over the years it got to a point that attempts to outdo all the rest before them made the elaborations almost ridiculous.

You may be asking yourself by this point, *how does this apply to me?* Well, as we look back at many of the ways these troops soothed their psyches, we discover the concept of being a short-timer was far from being an act of simple amusement—it was truly a necessary part of the transitional process. It was sheer evidence of how creative humans can adapt and maintain hope that something different would come about, even while experiencing adverse conditions. This syndrome was a pressure valve invented by survivors to relieve long-endured amounts of stress.

In prior wars, there was no such thing as being a short-timer. During WWII, everyone was deployed for the duration of the war; there was no Date Eligible for Return from Overseas (*DEROS*). Servicemen and women only returned home early if their wounds dictated they could no longer remain in the combat theater. These warriors had to devise other ways to feel better about their predicament. So the WWII troops had the fortunate process of returning home by sea. They had fellow troops around them for weeks, at which time they had the opportunity to process their wartime memories. They were also able to feel their emotions, which ranged from anger to grief to joy and more. The other warriors were there to support them and provide witness to their combat experiences. They were in good and familiar company, which afforded them the safety needed to express themselves in whatever manner was best for them. Dark humor was, and still is, an effective coping skill used to make light of painful memories or experiences that are difficult to recall without an emotional buffer in place.

Presently, with the War on Terror, the troops find little solace in the idea of a "short-timer." For them, it can only have a temporary meaning. Sure, the troops become excited as they count down the days, hours and minutes before they return back to the States, but until the war is over, the reality of multiple rotations looming on the horizon offers little closure. Unless a warrior's enlistment is up and discharge is imminent, being "short" means very little to our military today. For those staying in for the long haul, other incentives (reenlistment bonuses, career promotions, etc.) suffice and help servicemen and women find a comforting salve for the inconveniences of ongoing deployments. The incentive program varies according to branch and demand for the skill in which men and women are trained.

I might add that for the present military, there is what I call a "reverse short-timer's syndrome." Marking off time seems to happen in reverse. Instead of marking off time in the combat zone, when they get home they begin marking off the days and hours until they are once again deployed.

Yet another observation with today's warriors is that some may even go out of their way to make problems right before being redeployed. This is done intentionally so that the moment of separation will not be such an emotional or painful experience. I have firsthand knowledge that some service people have even gone so far as to provoke a fight with either their partner or other family members. They intentionally create a sour note to justify "feeling better" about leaving again. One young soldier told me that he would provoke a fight and leave his wife so she could deal with the problem and not him. He said that he had more important things to deal with once he got to the sandbox. This is certainly not a loving way to leave the home front or create a supportive situation that will sustain during the long months apart. It is easy to see that this undoubtedly has serious long-term consequences on relationships.

Survival in a war zone is quite a feat in itself, and survival of relationships on the home front is no easy task either. Therefore, it is very important to learn how to express emotions in order to not leave a wake of destruction that could go unhandled for months at a time. (See Chapter 9, "Positive Steps in Coming Home".)

CHAPTER THREE

Between Deployments

They thought they would just keep waiting and waiting and never fight again. It was, of course, a dream, a hope, and for many of them, a prayer.
— Gary Paulsen, *Soldier's Heart*

Have you ever spent a night in bed and gotten up the next day not knowing whether or not you had slept? Maybe your mind was a bit hazy, and you could not get the previous evening out of your thoughts. It may have been as if you were in a place where time stood still and the days just melted into the next, a state of disconnect. There was no past, no future, and the present was too dreamlike to be real. The revolving door of one deployment after another can be very similar in the psyches of our military personnel.

Multiple deployments have caused some war-weary troops to live in that dreamlike state. Their time at home (between deployments) can become a surreal period, and they find it difficult to explain this to those who are closest to them. I have had warriors tell me, in confidence, that coming home was hardly worth the effort of packing their bags. Some of these warriors have also expressed being ashamed because they secretly wished to be back in the war zone rather than be at home. The war zone is where they feel "at home" with their fellow comrades, with people who can relate to them and their way of thinking. They don't have to explain why they are acting or feeling a certain way. They have told me that they have fewer decisions to make when they are down range and life in the sandbox is often much easier. The expectations are clear and structured, but when they get back to the home front, they feel like they can no longer relate to other people as they did before they were deployed. The responsibilities of having to interact with civilians and be accountable to their loved ones may leave them feeling overwhelmed..

Those of us who have never gone to war will never understand or even imagine in our wildest dreams what these men and women have gone through. However, we can do our best to see the world through the shade of their lenses. By doing so, we may gain a more complete perspective of why it is hard for them to be around people and how they have grown beyond their chronological age.

For example, they leave as young, "green" service members, and they return as seasoned warriors. They may be young in age, but in their soul they are quite mature; their innocence has been lost. It is important for servicemen and women to find a way to come together and reinvent their relationships in order to start over again. It is a great opportunity for couples to rediscover one another, to strive to work as a team, and to build empathy, compassion and respect. This is done by communicating with each other and opening themselves up to seeing both perspectives.

On an interesting note, some family members have reluctantly shared with me that they wish their warrior would stay away until they could come home for good. The transitional period can certainly be disruptive to our warriors as they try to keep their edges sharp for future combat situations. They do this because they know they will be returning to the war zone at a moment's notice. This fact is etched in their minds, and to let down and deal with dynamics at home can interfere and leave them less conditioned for future deployments.

On the other hand, families sometimes feel that their system at home is disrupted by a warrior's return, and the pressure of maintaining a comfortable atmosphere leaves them walking on eggshells. So both sides are struggling to put these perspectives together in a way where each gets his or her needs met without creating an atmosphere of hurt and distance. Of course, as with everything else I cover in this book, there are exceptions and variations to almost every scenario.

Most men and women home on leave live in a quandary of having two "faces" that seem to compete for dominance. They long to be home, but because they know they will have to go back to war, many feel they should not have come home at all. They want to remain with their fellow troops and get the job done, and they sometimes feel that due to their absence, something bad will happen down range. There is a great sense of responsibility and commitment to their fellow warriors. But when this thinking is present, they live with a sense of guilt that they may be letting their families down too. The emotional torment can result in several major signs of combat operational stress, such as guilt, anxiety, social withdrawal, anger, excessive alcohol use, sleep disruption and depression.

A good friend of mine has a grandson in the Marine Corps who is on his second tour in Iraq. Before arriving home after his first deployment, the family received a letter from the commanding officer outlining some key do's and don'ts. This is not a bad idea, and hopefully more commanders will be as sensitive to the many transitional challenges that affect today's troops. However, in this same letter, another message was spelled out, almost between the lines.

The company commander clearly instructed the family to avoid doing anything that would divert this young man's attention away from his duty as a warrior. He was essentially reminding this Marine not to get too comfortable with civilian pursuits while stateside because it could be detrimental to his ability to function once he is redeployed. In other words, as in the samurai code, keep your edge sharp, and don't let your guard down.

The bottom line is that these military leaders are responsible for their men and women in uniform, and they take it personally when they lose one of their warriors. They want their troops to be combat ready and focused on their mission until the task is completed and they are back on home soil. This requires effort from all fronts, even from those at home.

Some of the troops I have counseled reported they felt anger while at home because they felt they had, in fact, become too comfortable, and they knew they were going to have to work extra hard to regain the tough demeanor of an effective warrior and be adequately responsive in the field.

How does one find respite in the middle of this kind of turmoil? Is this young warrior not able to get a breather? Or is he or she to be wired tight all the time while at home to ensure that he/she does not become a casualty in the war zone? Leaders know how vital it is for their war fighters to be emotionally fit for the task at hand. Even the leaders themselves are caught in a difficult spot, as they have stress symptoms themselves. The leaders must retain a stoic exterior in order to set the stage for their men and women in uniform, but the cost can be high and far reaching. What is missing here is the fact that they are, quite simply and surely, becoming casualties anyway—but not easily identifiable ones, as some wounds are invisible and many will suffer in silence.

By not being allowed to stand down after a combat tour, the warrior is becoming a casualty of the soul. Ideally, what is needed most after the long, harrowing months in the combat zone is the opportunity to just let down, relax and be immersed completely in the things that bring enjoyment. These things may vary for each person. The more that family and loved ones at home prepare for the homecoming and reduce demands, expectations, and distractions, the more likely the family time will be restful and a sanctuary in the midst of this time of transition.

Readiness

The dictionary definition of *readiness* is "**a:** prepared mentally or physically for some experience or action; **b:** prepared for immediate use."

With this in mind, I would like to also support the Marine commander's intention. He is doing his best to have his warriors maintain a certain level of readiness when they are not engaged. In his mind, he is keeping them sharp so they can return to their job with the level of focus that is required to be an asset and not a liability on the battlefield.

It is important for those at home to know that one of the most vulnerable times for a warrior in a war zone is the comedown after experiencing a "deployment high." This high takes place during times of a deployment when things escalate to a peak. There is a lull in the action for most—others remain hypervigilant to ensure that it truly is a time of relative inaction—but the downside and danger associated with this is complacency. Many warriors have trouble getting back into the groove of the war itself once this period is over, and complacency can be a killer in a combat zone.

Key holidays (Christmas, New Years Day, etc.) can usher in these highs. During the Vietnam War, Christmas and New Years Day, as well as the Lunar New Year (*Tết*) for the Vietnamese, were such times. Cease-fires were called, but according to the troops, it became an eerie time of mistrust on both sides, and they actually went on super-alert.

If we understand a homecoming after serving in Iraq and/or Afghanistan to be a deployment high, and we recognize that redeployment is probable, we can understand the importance of helping our warrior not lose his or her edge between deployments. At the same time, we must begin to walk hand in hand with that reality and investigate ways to insert some rest, fun and general slack-off time into their daily routines once they are home. It is a challenge worth putting much time and effort into accomplishing.

In order for this to happen, partners and families must abandon their expectations. They must allow their warrior the freedom to do what they feel they must do within the parameters set by the specific relationship. For parents, this means not demanding time curfews or limiting social interactions. I have heard many stories of families who had plans for redecorating their warrior's room. One family even allowed the younger brother to toss out "junk" (things he didn't want or need) in his deployed brother's room. My advice is to leave it all alone! Don't mess with their belongings.

Another point is to respect their decision-making process in matters of their home environment. To remove and change the setting leaves them little familiarity and predictability. Some Vietnam veterans, as well as current troops I know, have told me that after they left for the war zone, some of their families had moved. When they returned, this new environment left them feeling as if they never really came "home."

For those of you who have a partner and children to return home to, it is critical that you communicate before you return back to the States. Make certain to discuss the clear importance of balancing time for yourself, your partner, and your children. It is important to nourish these connections and spend quality time together as a family. Remember to nourish your primary relationship if you are in a partnership, and leave all others until you have spent time together. This even goes for those with children; be sure to secure adult time together with your mate, away from family obligations. In order to do this, you must let your partner know your limitations. Make sure the time you do have together is quality and that you can take breaks from any demands when necessary without feeling guilt or resentment. Planning for this is everything!

Recently, while at an airport in a city where many military families reside, I observed a family with three children—a baby girl about eighteen months old, a three-year-old son, and a seven-year-old daughter. The mother watched the two older children while the father held the youngest. The father was not speaking to the eldest daughter or to his wife. It was obvious he was a soldier by the adornments he sported. When he did communicate to his eldest daughter, he used hand signals and was stern and very demanding in his presentation. Apparently they were in the midst of some issues, and each parent was disconnected from the other, but they still maintained a connection to their children. Unfortunately, many couples forget to pay attention to the adult connection, but this is the glue that holds the family together. For the family to remain alive and vibrant, it is vital for the parents to be intact in their relationship.

The particular Marine commander I mentioned before was a professional, and the troops' best interest was in his hands. In order to remain combat ready, it was important for him to make those around him aware of the liabilities that result from losing the edge one needed to do one's job and survive in combat. I cannot, or would not, in any way dissuade my readers to do anything *but* stay ready for their jobs ahead, because I know the importance of maintaining such sharpness. However, what I also know is how important it is for a human being, especially one who endures the tremendous stress of war, to find a time and place to soothe the soul. One needs to strike a balance between readiness and relaxation. That is the challenge, and it is a most important one to manage.

For the warrior: When, or before, you get home, communicate to your loved ones your desire and need to spend time working out, studying tactics, upgrading your gear, or whatever else you do to maintain readiness. Let them know ahead of time that you need to keep yourself ready to be a warrior once again in the future, and that you need time with your comrades. What you are doing is showing your loved ones and friends that you care about them, and you are giving them notice not only that you will be doing this, but that it also generally does not include them. This is a courteous gesture and will be much appreciated. As difficult as it may be, you must also keep in mind how spending most of your free time away from your family will affect your relationship.

For the loved one(s): Practice your own form of readiness. Do your homework and find out as much as you can about how a warrior stays ready. When your warrior gets home, communicate to them that you know they have the need and desire to stay fit and ready to return to military duty. Ask if there is anything you can do to help them come up with a good schedule and strike a reasonable balance between readiness time and family time. By creating this balance, you will come to a healthy meeting of the minds and avoid many hardships and misunderstandings that can happen between deployments. For the adventurous spouse or child, perhaps even asking to work out with your warrior from time to time could be both fun and bonding. (It is amazing how many of these troops enjoy showing others what they have learned to stay in shape and survive while on military duty.) The objective is to respect each other and find a mutually comfortable way to nourish your relationship as well as your individual pursuits.

CHAPTER FOUR

How Souls Become Casualties of War

He felt alone now. Always alone. He existed in a world
that he believed—no, he knew—would end for him soon.
                    – Gary Paulsen, Soldier's Heart

I believe that the more warriors and loved ones can learn about what seem to be peculiar attitudes and behaviors (but which are really normal) after experiencing combat, the more equipped they will be to make healthy transitions and be better prepared for the next deployment. It is with this view in mind that we briefly view another level of how war impacts our men and women in uniform.

I work as a professional, and I have a doctorate in clinical psychology, but I do not profess to be a theologian. The term *soul* is important in this writing, but I do not bring it up in a religious way. I use the idea of a *soul* for the lack of a better term to describe the inner workings of people being impacted by their circumstances in life—the thought processes, rationalizations, justifications, choices and emotional experiences surrounding these events.

Many of us struggle to formulate meaning and purpose throughout our lives. The soul is nourished by this search for meaning, but it can also be torn apart if meaning cannot be found or if one's perception of reality stands in contradiction to one's belief systems or view of oneself.

As souls going about our life here on earth, we blossom as social beings. That is a self-evident truth apparent in most humans. We thrive on being among other souls, and the more we have in common with them, the closer we desire that association to be. It is unusual for a person to want to have nothing to do with the rest of humanity or to choose to go into complete isolation merely upon a whim. Yet the heavy-impacting results of a war on the human psyche have a tendency to drive people away from others. The very nature of something as difficult or life-altering as war sometimes causes an inclination toward isolation. Such isolation can certainly work against someone who is struggling with wartime memories, but on the other hand, it can offer solace in the wake of such emotional turmoil. I want to point out that isolation and avoidance can be a form of self-care if done in small increments. However, if these behaviors overpower your desire to be connected with your support systems and those around you, then this is something to be addressed and reevaluated.

We are pack animals by nature, and we seek out associations and a sense of belonging with those with whom we feel an inner connection. As a warrior bonds with another in an adverse situation, these connections are particularly strong and the souls meld together at a time of need like no other. Warriors literally commit to lay down their lives for their fellow comrades. These bonds are sometimes difficult for loved ones and family members to understand and accept, and they may often feel left out.

This concept is mirrored in the animal kingdom when two very different creatures bond under adverse conditions. Following the tsunami in Southeast Asia, a tortoise and a baby hippopotamus formed a very close caretaking relationship with each other after they were separated from their biological families. This was a very unlikely match from those of us looking in, but to them it was extremely significant and essential to their survival.

As we consider the primal urge for souls to receive nurturing through connections with other souls, we can also easily see the flip side. When these ties are broken through the engagement of wartime duties, over time, this nurturing is disrupted and can sometimes cease to exist entirely. So relationships with those on the home front can easily become casualties of war if not recognized and given attention. In order to maintain and nourish these relationships, it is vital that there be mutual recognition and validation for the efforts put forth to be kind. We so often miss the signals or fail to interpret attempts to connect with each other. Finding mutual activities or a common base, such as faith, or spirituality, does wonders in bringing people closer to the core of their relationships.

For warriors, it happens like this: A human being goes to fight in a war zone (by the way, survivors of natural disasters or terrifying physical assaults may experience similar manifestations). As the confusion and shock of the impact decreases, they begin to realize that they have gone through something beyond a "normal" or usual, everyday life experience. (I have had many patients tell me that it was all so unreal that it seemed to have never happened—but they know it did.) In their soul, they have traveled into the dark and witnessed things that most people on the outside would consider inconceivable. In other words, the shadow side of a person emerges when exposed to various aspects of war. This is a normal and expected process.

When one steps back and is no longer in a situation that requires total focus, such as duties in the war zone, they come to realize what has occurred. Sometimes these realizations are very difficult to incorporate into how they define themselves, so when that happens, a duality comes into focus. One side is of a warrior who has walked a path that may have not coincided with his or her self-view, and the other is the perception that others bestow upon the warrior as being a "hero" . These two perspectives can be at odds and can leave the warrior feeling conflicted internally.

It is during this phase of the trauma that most survivors convince themselves that no one else could ever understand what they have gone through. They develop a need to mask these aspects from others who have not walked in their boots. In the war zone, it was necessary for survival to separate themselves emotionally from the experience. Our warriors know that there is just no way that their civilian counterparts will ever truly comprehend what they have experienced. Even for our troops, there are often no words in our vocabulary to adequately convey their story.

These warriors have been living on the edge, fully engaged with life on many levels, experiencing the intensity of daily doses of adrenaline, and they have done their wartime jobs incredibly well for months while down range. Upon coming home, they see that their friends and families just don't "get it". The warriors ask themselves, "*is this all there is?*" and wonder if anyone has a clue about what life was like for them.

I can see much of this on a personal level, certainly not to the degree of being in combat, but by being on the road and embedded with the troops right out of combat day in and day out. This experience has exposed me to many incredible stories of those in and out of the war zone that have brought significant meaning to my life. People sometimes ask me, "What it is like to be with the troops?" This question leaves me speechless because the personal experience is extremely intense and rewarding, but they would never understand. It is like seeing a helium balloon flying high and witnessing it leaking slowly. When it no longer contains enough helium to hold it up in the air, the balloon fizzles and flattens. Those who did not see it flying high can only view the aftermath: a deflated, lifeless form. Since this is an area where there is an obvious disconnect between our troops and their loved ones, we must accept that there will be some level of misunderstanding. But coming together as a community of support is still possible and much needed.

The warrior must realize and accept that those at home will not be able to relate to their down range experience. The realities of the warrior and family members have become different. It now requires that both you and your loved ones focus on other aspects in your relationships that are still strong and connected with what is reality for you both. One important thing to remember is that "reality" is merely something that you and others can agree upon. If another person has no clue where you have been, or what you have done, then there is not much that can be communicated or agreed upon. Find topics and interests that you all know something about. You know war, but your family does not, so focus on what is strong in the union and bring it out to create a more unified experience.

Many warriors lose the desire to open up for fear they will be judged, and they worry that this may be used against them in the future. Some feel they do not want to take away the innocence of their loved ones or have them carry their burden. The effect of this type of coping further isolates them emotionally and sets them aside from others. This way of thinking gives them justification for keeping these experiences to themselves or just "stuffing it", thinking that it will go away. In reality, these memories can eat away at one's soul over the days and years to come. Stuffing it will only make it worse.

When they make the decision to pull away, this is the first step away from intimate contact with other souls. Needlessly, it is their own inner self that becomes the casualty of the experience. (I say "needlessly" because much of the remedy is relatively uncomplicated, and many times it becomes a simple process of exploring the experience by talking it out—telling your story—and discovering some lasting resolutions and alternatives to isolating due to the trauma.)

It has been said that a good author does not tell you something new; they merely say something that you have known all along but never had the right words to express it. Movies can sometimes do the same thing. A Vietnam veteran friend of mine was struck suddenly with a realization about isolation and PTSD after watching a certain scene in the movie *Saving Private Ryan*. The star, Tom Hanks, plays the part of a schoolteacher in civilian life who had become an officer, a Ranger captain, due to his level of education. As the scene unfolds, we see the young captain after he has just led his men up the bloody sand dunes of Omaha Beach. Once they have cleared the bunkers of enemy soldiers, and there is a lull in the action, he sits down on some sandbags. Laying his helmet aside, he says, "every time I shoot someone, I get farther away from home." My friend told me that the movie could have ended right there and he would have been satisfied—that statement put into words what he (my friend) had been mentally wrestling with for decades, and now he had finally heard his feelings expressed in one sentence that said it all.

This "farther away from home" feeling illustrates how a wounded soul feels when he or she isolates and turns away from those he or she knows and loves. In other words, the further one gets from their core by shutting down emotionally and deciding that no one else could understand, the lonelier their world becomes.

It is the separation from self, or who you are and how others have perceived you to be, that is most difficult, and now you may struggle with who you *think* you have become. However, looking at the positive side of change clearly allows you to recognize and, more importantly, accept these changes as strengths and areas of growth in your life.

As foreign as it may seem to those who have seen the worst times—especially in a war where so many basic values seem to vanish—growth does happen. Recently, I threw out a question to a group of troops that had just returned from the war zone. I asked them to tell me something that they had learned about themselves while down range. One young man said to me that he now can see how he has to slow down and really see the beauty in the world he has returned to. He went on to say that he cannot take things fore- granted like he used to. Now he has learned to see the importance and value he has been taught and the value of those relationships he has formed both in the military and at home. His wartime experience allowed him to see what was really important now and that he could see life from a different perspective because of his experiences in the war zone. Another soldier said that he looked out his window and saw a tree ladened heavily with snow and the branches were bent nearly to the ground. He then said "that tree now represents me and my resiliency. I know now that I may bend, and my branches may get very heavy with the weight of life, but I will never break."

These are two examples of how having been exposed to war from many perspectives allowed these two warriors to see the gifts that were bestowed upon them. They accepted who they have become and have accepted the positive aspects of such an impacting transformation.

Without getting too philosophical, I know that out of the rough comes finely cut gemstones, which makes it even more important that you continue to search for all the positive aspects of where you have been and where you are now.

This also goes for those on the home front. Change is inevitable, but it does not have to be something negative. It gives us opportunities to challenge ourselves beyond what we thought were our self-imposed limitations.

As the symptoms associated with trauma begin to surface, which can be delayed for many post-incident years, the survivors of trauma can find themselves feeling more and more alone. They may live with their secrets, believing that no one could ever understand what they have experienced. In order to maintain themselves and perhaps save others the misery of having to hear about their trauma, they keep their distance (physically, emotionally, or both) from the world around them. But as a result, their soul suffers the consequences—and the worst part of it is, those who know and love them also suffer from that same isolation as well. Their loved ones may shut down themselves so as not to feel the pain of losing that part of their warrior and the relationship.

Without love, we humans shrivel. The unloved child, the neglected infant, will almost surely die on many levels. The same goes for those adults who think they have become unloved due to the ugly stains that war has marked them with. They may have seen the worst in their fellow man, and they may have endured and participated in horrible events. They may be convinced that loving someone

like themselves would be the greatest of all double stan-
dards, and they would not expect (or demand) the world
to love them any longer—so they place themselves in emotional exile. I have heard this many times: "I am not worthy
of love."

Some of the warriors I work with truly feel that they are
not worthy of love. A part of their soul feels tainted, and
they worry that if they get too close to people, others will
see this in them as well. They are forever changed by their
experience in the war zone, some more than others, because
of a wide array of variables: duties, levels of resiliency, life
experience, background, ways of coping, cultural influences,
and personality traits, to name a few. This answers the question of why we are both affected and respond so differently;
no two people are the same.

In conclusion, it is important to realize that love is the
source and creator of life. I am certain that with enough
love, even the deepest wounds can be healed. Love is the
"juice" that sustains you while in combat, and it is what
compels you to go the extra mile. It is the force that drives
our decisions in many directions throughout life—love is
the essential power that deepens our relationships. If you
work hard to understand this, you will be able to reap the
rewards for yourself and those around you. Community is
what you have fallen upon, and you are not alone in this
journey. We have learned lessons from the wars of the past.
If we look at the Vietnam conflict, we see that our warriors
went alone and came back alone, and this is one of the de-
fining moments that forever changed many of our Vietnam
veterans' lives. Sometimes you may not feel as if you have a
community who loves and cares about you, but you do,
and in order to receive, you must open yourself up to taking the risk of reaching out. It is always understood that

there are many things about your experience you may never talk about, and I hope that loved ones will always respect these boundaries and not demand that you tell it exactly the way it was. This is a delicate situation that requires patience and respect on all fronts.

Writing and talking about the past will most likely require small steps on your part. So share your story, but do it with a trusted veteran or loved one, and know that it will be worth the effort (and, perhaps, the risk).

CHAPTER FIVE

Reinforcing the Ramparts of Your Relationship

...and if she had known what was to come of it, if she had known and could tell him what would come of it, she would have fought to drag him back and let the federal government keep their eleven dollars a month.
— Gary Paulsen, *Soldier's Heart*

With each deployment, warriors and families will experience differences in their relationships. It is impossible to say exactly how your loved one will be feeling when they return. Everyone has a different resiliency and tolerance level to hardships. I can, however, give you a combination of signs along the trail. These are "red flag" warnings that come from some actual experiences of veterans from earlier wars.

The very first thing you need to do is prepare yourself mentally for the changes and differences that will prevail in your relationship. As much as we all want things to go back to the way they were *before* deployment, you must realize that this is an unreal expectation. To think that you and your loved can go back to square one and pick up where you left off is setting yourself up for loss and disappointment. Time has passed and lives have changed. Be progressive and realistic, and stay focused on the here and now. We can easily get lost in the past recalling how life once was, but this does little good when working through an issue that is impacting us presently. This is a time to reinvent and reassess yourself and your relationships. As I have mentioned before, out of change comes growth. I challenge you to look inside yourself and recognize these changes for what they are and then adapt them into your new life.

Change

Listed below are some ways that we have seen returnees change because of exposure to the hardships and dangers of war. (Remember, some of these changes may seem unreal or trite to you, but if your loved one is reacting to them, they become issues to be recognized and addressed.) It is never a good idea to do this alone. The support of others is essential, and most partners and/or family members have found that being connected to a support group and a community helps immensely.

As each deployment occurs, the security of a team becomes more and more vital. When getting together, it may be a good practice to discuss what possible methods can be planned out in order to cope with the inevitable changes in productive ways. Brainstorming with people who find themselves in similar situations is an extremely important and powerful component to coping and healing. We learn from others and their trials and tribulations, and this, in turn, will save you a great deal of time during your journey.

With each deployment, your warrior will most likely develop some quirks or habits that may make them seem different. You must realize that these have been acquired mostly as a means of physically surviving or caring for themselves emotionally while in the war zone. It is important for you to know that these behaviors have been infused by the war and that they have little to do with how your loved one feels about you. Here are some common changes to look for.

Your warrior:

- Is still focused or preoccupied with his or her military readiness and cannot seem to disconnect from this mindset in order to enter into peace, love and spending quality time with loved ones.
- Is now quiet and over-reflective (perhaps they just want to "chill" with a cold beer, a TV remote control or a video game).
- Is now nervous and jumpy at the slightest provocation.
- Is now overly sensitive to sights, sounds and situations that are reminders of the war zone.
- Is now short-tempered and becomes easily frustrated or angry over seemingly small matters.
- Cannot tolerate simple mistakes made by those around him or her.
- May shut down due to emotional overload in an effort to isolate and/or avoid life.
- May have a defensive "perimeter wire" in place preventing anyone from getting too close to them. (They may have made a subconscious vow to not get too close to anyone because they fear it will be too painful when they lose them.)
- Sleeps with the lights or TV on all night, sleeps on the floor or on the couch, or cannot sleep. They may be up and down all night long checking the "perimeter," or they may have nightmares.
- Must have all the doors open inside the house at all times or may demand that the doors remain closed as a barrier.

- Sleeps with, or has weapons nearby to feel safe and armed.
- Is overly concerned with safety, but may get upset when this notion is brought up.
- May have bouts of road rage.
- Practices aggressive posturing with heated discussions. They may be quick to ignite!
- Excessively consumes alcohol, energy drinks, recreational and/or prescription drugs or caffeine (self-medication).
- Sits in "strategic" locations in public places to detect and be alert for sudden enemy attacks. (Allow them to always have their back to the wall in restaurants. It will make for a much more peaceful experience for you both.)
- May not want to unpack the clothes they brought back from the war zone. (Too many reminders may be in the duffle bag or they may have the feeling they will be called back and need to have things packed and ready to go at a moment's notice.)

It is important that you do your part in exploring these and other aspects that you see in your warrior and gain an understanding of how these behaviors are the result of wartime experiences or training. If you are lucky enough to be part of a support group, bring these issues up and discuss how you can cope with them in a productive way.

Reminder: It is to your advantage to educate yourself on the signs of post-traumatic stress disorder and/or combat operational stress. The more you know and can make quality determinations about these issues, the better equipped you will be to help in the recovery process of those you care about. Here is a very small list of the most common behaviors to be watchful of:

- Being haunted by memories of the war
- Always feeling like they're on guard
- Trouble with irritability and anger
- Isolating themselves from others
- Preoccupied with television or video games
- Having nightmares that disrupt their sleep
- Drinking more than usual (self-medicating)
- Suicidal or homicidal comments

Reinforcements

Here are some ways that you can help reinforce your relationship.

- Practice open communication. Share that you understand the importance of their being ready for military duty and suggest times and schedules so that there is a satisfactory balance between this need and having quality time together.
- Give your warrior plenty of space and time. Let them chill and even help them to do that. They are emotionally, spiritually and physically exhausted.
- Create a special place in the house just for them. Make sure they have a sanctuary that others cannot invade unless invited.
- *For partners:* Plan to start the dating process all over again. Rekindle the friendship first, then the romantic aspects of your relationship will fall into place.

- Some of you may find that you feel uncomfortable or even frightened with intimacy. Take it slow and proceed at a mutually agreed pace. (Remember, this is also communication.)
- Plan to get involved in activities together.
- Show that you appreciate their effort to be involved; give them recognition and love.
- Sort out the responsibilities of household duties, spending and child rearing later.
- *For family members:* Plan to view the relationship in the present and avoid trying to relive childhood activities, remembrances and/or dreams. (After engaging in wartime activities, dreams and innocent notions of life may have been shattered and are most likely the furthest thing from their minds. Bringing up the memories of their past can remind them too much of what they have lost.) This is particularly true for the parents of our warriors.

Re-enforce some creative ways to be sensitive to your loved one's idiosyncrasies. For example, it is considerate to ask them where *they* would like to sit in a restaurant or a theater. It is not unusual for them to also feel uncomfortable in social settings, so if you want to have a social gathering to honor them, have it at someone else's home so your warrior can leave at any time without calling attention to themselves. Please check with your service member about what they want. It is not about what others want; it is about what your warrior wants and needs. It will mean a lot if they are given a choice in even what may seem like a small matter to you. Refrain from demanding that they go shopping in crowded malls or stores. Get creative. Leave your warrior outside the store or at home. Go on off hours when there are less people around. Be sensitive and this will really go a long way toward creating a positive outcome. Do what you can to keep the kids from crawling on them too much. Those who have been in a war zone inevitably will string an imaginary barrier like a "perimeter wire" to maintain their own safe space. Do not take it personally if your loved one does not hug you as much as you would like. In the war zone, touch is usually not a pleasant experience, and sometimes they bring this feeling home with them, so give it time! If you give them space by understanding and what the "wire" concept is all about, they will hopefully draw in closer over time at their own pace. (The "perimeter wire" principle is explained in detail in my other book, *Once a Warrior: Wired For Life*.

Take it slow. This is a journey, not a destination!

Writing It Down: A Good Thing to Do

In the middle of the storm, I realize it is difficult to keep track of your thoughts or those things you would like to communicate to your partner. This advice is for both the warrior and for the loved one at home. For the warrior, I highly recommend that you consider keeping a journal throughout each deployment. Writing helps put emotions into perspective, and it can give your partner an idea of what you were thinking and feeling while you were gone. Letter writing, e-mailing, and even phone calls do not always communicate fully what you are thinking each day. However, as one recently returning sergeant observed, too much communication can be stressful as well, because it has a tendency to cause the loss of focus for troops in the field. Find out what works for both you and your warrior. For the partner at home, you can include a section or keep a separate notebook for notes about financial and life decisions you made during the deployment. For the engaged warrior, it is not always convenient to write out an entire letter or make a phone call, but to keep a record of even the smallest emotion or thought will mean so much once you get back home. Writing it down can also help you know how to act the next time. You will know what worked well and what did not, and the detail will remind you of what you need to do to prepare so that next time will be easier.

Reminder: The military has always had its own means of communication, and many times civilians struggle to perceive the meanings. Recently I had an experience that I would like to share. I have a friend who is in the military, and I would write to him from the depths of my soul as I could relate on many levels. When (and if) I got a reply, it would be in one-word replies such as "awesome" or "great." As a result of working with the military for a while, I understand that this type of communication is more the norm than the exception. It is the nature of communication within the military arena. Even though these one-word responses were succinct from the soldier's point of view, they said it all for him. But left me feeling empty and feeling as if he had not even acknowledged my communication. This was certainly a misperception on my part, and it has taken me some time to understand that even though his response was brief, he had indeed read my postings. Now that I have this new understanding, I am no longer concerned with this response pattern. It is considered the "norm" rather than the exception.

This personal story illustrates how important it is that we communicate clearly and with enough substance that the other person feels validated, but without over communicating. However, the aspects of over communicating or speaking with too many words can also be a trigger for many of the warriors I know. They are accustomed to concise, short bursts of communication. If you are speaking with them and you go on and on,(ramble) they may quickly lose interest in what you are saying. They get it quickly, and prefer "just the facts, ma'am". Some of you may feel that your warrior is not listening to you, but he or she may simply be on overload by the amount of words you use, so keep it short, sweet and to the point. Hopefully this will help improve your communication patterns and create a better understanding between you. For fun, you may even invent some new acronyms to use in your personal vocabulary.

CHAPTER SIX

Warrior Up

There'd be a shooting war... if a man didn't hurry he'd miss it. The only shooting war to come in a man's life and if a man didn't step right along he'd miss the whole thing.
                                    – Gary Paulsen, *Soldier's Heart*

I have written this specifically for the warrior who has finished serving multiple tours and now is setting his or her sights on redeployment, a military career, or perhaps to leave the military entirely. It is an extension of the transitional information and course work that I provide for the military and veterans I work with all over the country.

There is a term used in writing called *takeaway value*, and it simply asks the question, "what certain features, points, views or specific information did this writing provide the reader with that they can take away and use productively when they finish the book?" (I say "productively" because there are some aspects of anything we learn that can be taken and used nonproductively as well.)

I would like to use that same term (*takeaway value*) in another way. I have renamed it so it will be more familiar to you as someone who has spent time in the military. I call it *secondary explosions*.

Remember: For every action, there is a reaction.

Secondary Explosions

One objective of ancient armies laying siege to a city or a fortification was to hang around long enough to either conquer or be paid a tribute if they stopped the attacks. A normal siege might last a few weeks or even months before surrender or a negotiated settlement could, or would, be worked out. This usually meant that a tribute of valuables would be paid by the besieged to pay off the army that has kept them surrounded for this time period. In many cases, the army would be paid and then move on, leaving the people poorer and less free but still possessing their independence.

Applying that scenario to the topic of being "besieged" by multiple deployments, as a warrior, you need to regroup and take stock in what you now possess as a result of your wartime military duty. What kickbacks are you now left with?

In combat situations, secondary explosions occur when engaged targets yield up the bonus of additional, sometimes hidden objectives. It is a "two for one", and there is nothing quite like the moment when a marksman aims at a target, hits it, and then experiences the exhilaration of a chain reaction of multiple explosions.

Our daily lives produce the same kind of secondary effects with either productive or destructive results. In almost everything we do, there seems to be an effect on our surroundings and circumstances—the ripple effect of what we do and think touches more than we are usually aware of. In other words, our actions create reactions, which may be ignored for a while but over time cannot be avoided. What we put out, we pull back in. It is a natural law of the universe that we live in. Good and bad alike will return to the initiator. However, without getting too much into the laws that govern our universe and the science of physics, I would like to draw on some other simple concepts affecting all of us as we travel along in life.

I have written this section with you in mind, and the topic of *secondary explosions* will contain some very special meanings for you. I hope this will make it easier to understand and apply.

The subject of secondary explosions fits well with the topic of how people stockpile past experiences in order to survive and succeed in today's world

There are some things—very important things—we learn in life that inadvertently get devalued, discarded or underutilized as time goes by. If we were to sit down and list out all the valuable lessons we experienced in a single lifetime (no matter how long or short), we would likely uncover a long-forgotten stash of important assets—assets that, if resurrected and used, could make a good life even better. Reminding ourselves of their usefulness is the core of this section.

The people in our current military, like so many veterans of past eras, are receiving many of those valuable assets today. Sadly though, most will go *the route most traveled* and settle for a belief that what they did in the military has little value in a civilian world. "Shoot, move and communicate" (watchwords and a basic military creed) is a classic example of how some of these hard-learned lessons can get relegated to trash heaps when military life comes to an end.

Shoot, move and communicate are foundational to what every soldier, sailor, coast guardsman, airman and Marine learns when becoming a team member in the defense of their country. It is a "military mantra" that guides our service people from the time they enter the military until they leave. By focusing on these three key elements and connecting relative meanings and examples, I have set out to emphasize the value and usage of those lessons. I did this as a means of hopefully making the overall concept more relatable and understandable.

Shoot

In my thirties, I began an academic journey that most people start in their early twenties. I aimed at a target and hit it, but the secondary benefits of my efforts are proving to be the dearest of all.

At the time, as a wife and new mother, I made a decision that changed the course of my life forever. I entered a master's program at a local university with the intention of obtaining my Ph.D. in clinical psychology. By setting my sights and honing my focus to complete this education, I finally earned my doctorate. However, at the time of finishing this lifetime goal, I never expected many of the residual rewards I have garnered since. The special moments as a therapist, teacher and writer I have experienced since graduating have afforded me precious opportunities to see aspects of peoples' lives that relatively few others ever do. If I had not aimed my desires and attention at arriving at this destination, as difficult as it was at times, most assuredly I would have missed targets I am now hitting.

Setting our sights on goals and achieving them is reward enough, but there is something quite breathtaking about the additional windfalls that can come along as a result of past experiences and efforts. On the other hand, if *we* never ignite a fire that sets off *our* dreams, those magical moments may never transpire. In other words, if a shot is never fired, a target will never be hit! It is all about "initiation".

With this in mind, let's take the subject of shooting and apply it to civilian settings. Letting go of an arrow, a bullet, a rocket, or another projectile (usually an article of war) is a proactive endeavor. Projection is the name of the game, and projecting ourselves into productive areas in life has a similar makeup. All we need to do is determine some of the more constructive aspects of the idea of shooting to accomplish some pretty amazing things. All it takes, without contradicting any of the valuable lessons learned while in the military, is to reframe some of your trained-in mindsets. You do this by connecting the dots that lead you from a combat shooting style over to more peaceful "missions" in civilian life.

An excellent place to start this connecting is to understand the actual framework of shooting and to make the correlation of *projecting* yourself into a post military lifestyle.

Advance or Defend

Success on a battlefield is dependent upon fire superiority. Understandably, shooting and maintaining weapons is the backbone of all basic training in the military. However, at first glance, transitioning military personnel can assume that this skill has no useful purpose in civilian life. After all, many warriors returning to the civilian sector do not seek careers requiring that sort of know-how (i.e. law enforcement, security, etc.). Most return to jobs that remove them far from their combat experiences.

Shooting is an action intended to penetrate. Its objective is to reach out and touch people and/or objects. It is not laid back, but is rather a highly proactive undertaking. By taking the idea of shooting and translating it to its positive usefulness in society, we can easily begin to see its intrinsic worth.

First of all, not much beyond the preservation of what you *have* is ever gained or achieved from a defensive attitude or position. Military experts have always recognized that skillful applications of a defensive operation can keep a military force from losing a war or a battle; however, they also agree that defense never wins a war. Only offensive operations ensure ultimate victory.

We must be active participants on this journey called life, not just passive bystanders. Take action! An unknown author once gave some good advice: "Life isn't about waiting for the storm to pass; it is about learning to dance in the rain."

With that in mind, we can get a good idea as to the value of being proactive. It is a confirmation that our assertiveness in relationships, careers, business or any other area of life is fundamental to attaining what we go after. We begin by recognizing that *we* are the ones responsible for the ultimate outcome, and waiting for something to happen or for someone else to do "something" is seldom a good strategy for achieving success.

Waiting has its noteworthy aspects and should be considered first in many dealings in life, but it is nearly always the one who steps out to make things happen who brings home the prize. If you feel the need to wait, the best "waiting" is that in anticipation of secondary explosions resulting from the penetrating fire you launched at targets at some previous time. It is a cause-and-effect universe. You can choose to be one or the other at any time.

Target Assessment: Ready and Responsible

As mentioned before, I was older in life when I set out on the quest for a doctorate in psychology. If I had thought in any way that I could not have attained my goal, I don't believe I would have even started. Before taking the leap, I did an in-depth appraisal of what was involved, and once I was confident that I could hit my target, I began the long process. I used whatever resources I could muster to see all the way to the end, and I made myself ready and responsible for any outcome—I did a target assessment before firing in the direction of the goal.

I did my homework before setting off on this voyage, and I tried to look at all the angles before jumping into a long-term endeavor. However, no one could have described the process to me, and it was a bit unnerving. Certainly nothing like going into combat, but it felt as if I was entering a war zone. I was faced with eight to ten years of struggle ahead of me just to complete the requirements for my rank. I knew that I had to go with my gut and do what I wanted regardless of how crazy people in my circle thought I was, or what I might lose. I was determined to give it my best shot.

At the time, I had a baby girl in tow, and every moment really had to count. They say you come into and out of this world alone, and the same thing is true for some of the goals we dream of pursuing. I had to rely on my internal motivation and just put one foot in front of the other while keeping the big picture in sight. There were also times when I imagined that it would be a straight shot, but

I found out this was far from true. There are always variables that cross our paths and, at many times, get in the way. I know how important it is to aim with the intention of hitting the targets, but I also found ways to cope when I did not hit them. It really boils down to maintaining commitment, vision, perseverance and self-discipline in order to achieve the goals we set forth. I can also tell you there were times when I thought I just could not go another step, but I pulled myself up by my bootstraps and kept my sights on my ultimate objective. I was bound and determined that nothing was going to take this opportunity away from me. I want to remind you that one baby step at a time is important. Surround yourself with people who believe in you and your dreams. Don't listen to the naysayers. Prove them wrong! I did it, and so can you, so never, never, ever give up! You have got to own it! When you entered basic training or boot camp, you may have thought at the time that it would have been easier to hang it up, but you stayed with it, and you persevered. For many of you, there is no way you would ever want to turn back the clock and not have had your military experience.

We are all of shortsightedness guilty at one time or another, and we often have to live with regretful consequences as a result. It is a known fact that shooters have different levels of culpability according to the proximity of their targets. A pilot dropping bombs from thousands of feet does may not experience the same level of feelings (i.e. regret, remorse, guilt or responsibility) that an infantryman who has just bayoneted an enemy soldier does. One creates destruction from a distance, while the other may never forget the warm blood that has stained his hands. However, those who see the before-and-after mental photographs are certainly affected by the visual impact of their duty. It becomes reality; this is why those who experience hand-to-hand or intense close-range fighting are impacted at a greater degree than those who are more physically removed while performing their warrior duties.

Due to the nature of their actions, marksmen notoriously do not assess the consequences. They are the cause; they project, and their targets receive. They seldom know the outcome of what they initiate, but on the other end, it is a different scenario completely. "Shooting" in a civilian endeavor is not like that. You may set your aim on a goal, then (for the best results) you must be able to project all the way down range before you squeeze off the round.

"Target assessment" is getting to know the ins and outs of a particular job before applying for it. Do your best to discover the intricacies of how a company expects its employees to dress or behave, or find out how to perform some skills needed for the position beforehand. Detailed target assessment leads you to do your "homework." It is one of the keys to success. Do a "recon" and obtain as much information as possible so you will be armed in advance before moving upon a position.

Weapon Familiarization

What are your weapons now? Taking the time to do a personal review and then tallying up all you have available is similar to the weapons familiarization classes you attended in your military training. Each skill or experience is a possible weapon, or tool, to use when seeking a solution to challenges in the civilian sector. They can be used in the process of reinventing yourself and educating those in your midst.

A familiarization checklist:

1. What are my natural talents?
2. What do I like doing?
3. What trained skills do I have?
4. How well do these skills translate into the civilian world?
5. Can I teach or can others benefit from my skills and experience?
6. With what I know and the resources I have, can I advance?

When making transitions from one life to another, especially a life that is clearly opposite to what we are familiar with, it is easy to lose sight of the usefulness of the skills and experiences we have stashed away in our arsenal. This is a very good reason to rely upon weapons familiarization. By linking your training and life experiences, you can now establish the connection between your current behaviors and your previous life. By doing so, you can better understand and determine the issues you are now confronted with. We do this by assessing and determining first and foremost exactly what the new situation is and how (or if) it can become a target with which to engage.

Remember to Breathe

In the military, before you were ever asked to shoot at a target, the task of getting to know your weapon and learning how to fire it was mandatory. These actions were all geared to make sure you could effectively engage a target when the time came. Right off the bat, you were taught and drilled on a couple of basic concepts: first, take up the slack in the trigger until it cannot move any farther to the rear without discharging; secondly, hold your breath; lastly, squeeze (don't pull) the trigger and discharge the weapon.

Let's now look at this in light of transitioning back into the ebb and flow of civilian life.

Zeroing Your Weapons

Everyone has their own patterns as they view life's targets through their individual sights. We all see what is down range in different ways. When a soldier is issued a new weapon, the first thing that must be done is to "zero" the sights. Zeroing is done on the shortest range, usually at twenty-five meters from a supported position, so as to most accurately engage the target; soldiers commence firing test rounds to adjust their sights until they are spot-on. When three rounds hit the target at a pattern the size of a quarter, it is zeroed. The weapon can then effectively be used to hit targets down range at one-thousand meters or more.

When you are making plans to engage a "target" (i.e. a job interview, a relationship, a presentation, or a certain project, etc.), it is necessary to zero the weapon you bring into play as you proceed. Perhaps you need to sharpen or revisit skills or information you have learned in the past, or maybe even upgrade your dress or styles to meet acceptance in an area you are approaching. I am not just talking about fashion sense here; I also mean the way you speak and handle yourself in the presence of people. It is sometimes difficult for warriors to be smooth in the heat of an interview or when dealing with your civilian counterparts. But be cool, and remember to breathe.

Your style of communication can certainly set the course. Be cautious of "commo" styles, which are perceived as gruff, curt or demanding. Humble yourself by using a confident, smooth and calm demeanor. Keep your cool! This will give you a much better chance to advance your likability and your goals.

It is a good idea to study and know your audience before you proceed. This will help you engage in conversation and feel more comfortable in the process so as not to be caught off guard or ambushed. Read up on a topic and study information about the target before you engage. You never want to be caught flat-footed, so hone your skills in whatever arena or "target" you intend to approach.

Move

Over the years I have found that when I just sit and wait for something to happen, it dawns on me that it is not always a good option. I usually have a hindsight realization that if I had just stepped out and been more proactive, my endeavors would have been more successful. The times when I did initiate moves, rather than sit still, my ideas or intended projects worked out for the best. This has actually proven itself many times, and I can vouch for the truth in the old saying, "It's easier to steer a moving car than one standing still." After spending several months at Schofield Barracks in Hawaii with the 25th Infantry Division, I now often refer to a point in time that equates to an opportunity for growth as, "I'm riding a wave, and I must catch it before it subsides."

I say all this to remind you that even in combat situations, the flexibility and ability to move is much more desirable than being pinned down. When you are fluid with your thinking and expressions, then attaining what you are looking for will come more easily. This way, I truly believe you become more open to receiving, and if you put that out there, it will come back to you. I am sure you who have been in the war zone can think of a few times when you wanted some action and you got it!

Transitions from military life back to civilian life, especially during wartime, can be thresholds packed with uncertainties. As one steps through the doorway and begins a journey of reentry into civilian life, the varied and sometimes unreal expectations can cause a person to get stuck or freeze up. First of all, remember that it is normal for this to happen. Secondly, you need to know it is perfectly fine not to succumb to the pressure dictating that you must do *something*. In fact, I highly recommend you step back for as long as you need to assess the terrain before traversing it—and don't do anything but rest, relax, and enjoy life as best you can. *But* do not get stuck there either! Tip: While you are taking the time to stand down and regroup, make every effort to *prepare to move out for the next objective*. Remember, we all need something we can hold on to and dream of, so don't sit back idly and settle for life to pass you by.

Many of the OIF and OEF troops whom I have had the honor of knowing and helping are uncertain as to what to do when they get home. Some will feel they need to go party with their buds and blow off a little adrenaline; but for those of you who have attended my workshops, we both know a steady diet of this can lead to trouble and a breakdown on many fronts of your life. After the initial celebratory time of returning back to your families and friends, it is time to chart your course in a new direction. Either you are gearing up for redeployment, preparing to PCS, or leaving the military—each of these activities has very different objectives. The Guard and Reservists are better prepared to take time off when they get home. This, however, this period of time can be very short, depending on how long they were deployed, and then it is back in the saddle—a predicament which certainly presents many challenges.

By the same token, I have also seen many a warrior flounder and feel lost, overwhelmed, and confused about what to do once they return to their civilian lives. It becomes difficult for them to know exactly what to do with the inactivity, lack of structure, unpredictable routine, loss of objectives, and the missing camaraderie to which they have been so accustomed. To reestablish these familiar components, it is your mission to simply move forward. I know this may not be an easy task, but it is necessary for you to take back your life.

In order to attain a goal (such as securing employment, an education, or whatever you desire), you have to embrace *change*. Clearly you have changed, and you need to once again make some changes adjustments, but this change will not happen automatically. If you sit around and wait for something to happen in your favor, it probably won't. You cannot be afraid to shake things up a little. On the battlefield, that is what you did best, so get out there, shake it up, and make it happen. Stepping out toward an objective in civilian life is not any different from being at war, and, as you probably have learned, fear can get you or a buddy killed. Fear can paralyze even the most seasoned of warriors, but you must do everything in your power to ramp it up and get past that emotion in order to minimize your losses. Keep charging forward. You are a warrior, and now you must be a warrior in *all* areas of your life. You have the skills, the determination, and the will; now put them to work for you in the civilian sector with your relationships, employment and any other objectives you may have.

Both good days and bad days are ahead, but dream a little, lighten up, and brainstorm. Be creative, set goals, and don't take "no" for an answer—and never, never give up! Warrior up! Be proactive like you know how to do—it is in your soul!

Communicate and Connect

Communication and connection is what keeps things together, especially in the twenty-first century. It is the one essential ingredient that bonds humans together and promotes understanding between us. Communication is a proven gateway to success, loving relationships, and all that is good in life, and it happens on many different levels. The interesting thing about it is that it is not just something that humans do to interact, it spans the entirety of most life forms on our planet. However, the ability to communicate in so many different modes is unique to us humans, and with the rapid upward spiral of technology, it is sometimes nearly impossible to keep up-to-date.

In combat, communication is a relatively refined art form primarily designed to eliminate potentially fatal misunderstandings. Transmitting the wrong signals, codes or coordinates can make the difference between life and death, victory and defeat. It is important to keep this in mind when you are traversing the span between military life and civilian life. Keep in mind also that communication is not only speaking words, but it is acting out and displaying body language as well.

In my work with veterans, active duty servicemen and women, and their families over the years, I have found that sorting out issues that need clarification remains the most challenging part of reintegration in most relationships. Once a person has had to experience (sometimes on a daily basis) communicating in the midst of extreme circumstances, certain habits form. As a warrior, these "habits" may have become useful ways of thinking and served as a means to survive. However, they may not translate well to your civilian counterparts. It is important to reevaluate and realize what "area of operation" you are now in, and then make concerted efforts to think about the context and delivery of what you intend to say (or do) beforehand.

Job interviews, family and personal relationship solidification, and even the simplest of social settings require a degree of good communication skills. However, you must understand that civilians may not get the gist of what you mean if you speak or act in ways that pertain only to military communication. As we mentioned in our book *Once a Warrior: Wired for Life*, it is important to learn the fine art of "re-behaving". Take it slow and steady. Civilian approaches will come back if you give it enough consideration and time. Remember, you were a civilian before you became a service member, so I know that capability is in there somewhere.

The military has its own way of communicating; it is usually in acronyms and very succinct and concise "bursts" for the purpose of transmitting vital information—just the facts—in the least amount of time for the most impact. This can mean the difference between life and death. It is urgent because you can never tell when the communication path is eliminated or damaged, and you may be left outside the wire without the backup you require to accomplish the mission or even come back alive.

Unfortunately, your family and friends may not have experienced this; they more than likely have never had to communicate under such extreme conditions. So this takes patience on your part, as well as understanding on theirs. Coming across the line from both perspectives will certainly enhance empathy and connection.

For the family at home reading this section: You can help. First of all, realize and accept that your warrior has been trained in ways of living that you are not familiar with. If what they say or do seems out of place or even overkill, remember that situations that appear relatively harmless to you may not carry the same meaning for your warrior. You must do your own conscious evaluation before responding (or reacting) to the methods of communication that seem so foreign to you. Do your best to understand that being overly verbal may not be one of your warrior's strong suits; he or she may not be very expressive in conversation. Most importantly, be compassionate and supportive. Don't put too much demand on them or you could push your warrior further underground. Finally, learn as much as you can. This will certainly help your warrior feel understood and respected, and you will reap the benefits of a reciprocal desire to learn about your life on the home front as well. Strong bonds and quality relationships are formed by coming together with the objective of obtaining a better understanding of each other's experiences.

When a miscommunication occurs, do what you can to ask yourself, *what was this all about?* Chances are, it is a reaction to something that may have been carried over from the war zone or a previous deployment. Over time, when trust and relating to each other has been reestablished, some of these things will sort themselves out. Patience is the key.

Stacking Arms

We have made it through the siege, and it is over. The threat has subsided, and it is time to take stock of what effects the experience has created. Damage assessment, supply (energy) depletion, regrouping to determine the rebuilding process, and noting the positive and valuable lessons learned are all part of the what I call "stacking arms".

What does one do with a rifle when it is not in use? The answer to this is "stack arms". Stacking arms is used for a unit of troopers to ground weapons in a uniform manner, and to keep them clean while taking a break from marching, drilling and fighting. It is an appropriate term for both warriors and loved ones to begin rebuilding their lives and making plans for the future.

The "stacking swivel" on a rifle (an M1 Garand) is used when three M1s are hooked together in the field so as not to allow them to fall over. Early firearms were hooked together by the ramrod or bayonet, but on more modern rifles, a C-shaped swivel, attached high on the barrel, facilitated the making of a stack. The stack was made strong by allowing two or three rifles to interlock while another was leaned against them.

I use the stacking swivel to illustrate the need for all of us to lock arms and remain united for the sake of our troops while this war continues to call them to foreign lands. None of us can stand alone, and the entire country is being affected daily by the revolving door of multiple deployments. When anger and spite are the only means with which we disagree about geopolitical circumstances, we have, as a society, created our "siege works". The heaps of dirt and debris that have been stacked against the walls during the long-standing siege will take too long to break down if we cannot forgive and forget. It is our choice to either surround ourselves with the pain and pessimism of the past or actively choose the positive and productive forward motion. It is up to us.

I hope that what I have shared here will serve to be the last rifle on the pile—the one that gives stability to the entire stack. My best to you as we all move along on this journey.

"I Got Your Six": A Gentle, But Concerned Reminder

Because the pressures of coming home from war can be very challenging at best, I have a responsibility to mention the very serious implications of losing hope and taking drastic measures as a result of not wanting to carry on. Yes, I am talking about suicide.

When I conduct my workshops with the troops, I stress the fact that you are all well trained to assess situations very quickly. I also know that you have had suicide awareness classes, etc.. However, there are a few additional items I would like to share from my perspective.

First of all, you are well trained to interpret communication patterns for your survival, and you undoubtedly know that about 70 percent of all communication is non-verbal. You have a good understanding of what voice tone, eye contact, and physical posturing mean. With this information, you can determine if what you are verbally being told aligns with the other aspects of communication you assess. On the other hand, you are a master of disguising your emotions because you do not want to "telegraph" to your enemy what is going on behind your eyes. You become battle-hardened and freeze your emotions in order to not give away any crucial information. Based on these two perspectives, you must continue to use these survival skills in order to watch your buddies around you. Even when you get home, you still need to remember "I got your six" and continue to cover one another's back.

If you get an intuitive feeling that something is not quite right and you notice the subtle nuances of change (for example, if your battle buddy is not going fishing with you as usual or not going for your weekly manicure together), then be proactive and do *something*. Do not sit back and wait until tomorrow, because tomorrow may never come. Know your protocol: Take your buddy to get help, see the chaplain, and notify the chain of command. Do not risk a life for the purpose of saving face.

The same thing goes with those on the home front. Remember that some of those on the home front may also be having some major issues as well. You must all take care of each other and take a very proactive stance on this topic. We all have a responsibility to make certain that we do what we must to ensure the safety of those around us.

PART TWO

CHAPTER SEVEN

For the Child

*"Plus they'll be paying me. I hear eleven dollars a month.
I'll send most of it home to you and Orren."*
*(The soldier is determine to send money home to his
mother and younger brother)*
                                        – Gary Paulsen, *Soldier's Heart*

*This is a very special section of this book for me. It is about
the children who are involved. If you do not have children, feel
free to skip over this section. However, almost everyone in the
military knows someone who has a child; therefore, it might be
a good source of information that you can pass along.*

The resiliency of the children in the matter of military
deployments and transitions certainly will depend upon the
resiliency of the family system. If there are loving interactions, strong bonds, and good communication in the family,
this can go a long way in sustaining the foundation for the
children involved.

It is quite easy to see that whatever is broken before a
deployment occurs will only get worse under the pressure
of the absence and the changes that occur if they don't
have what it takes to bring it back together. Kids, unfortu-

nately, are the ones who are the recipients of their parents' pain and angst. The cycle of child abuse is at least two times greater in families with deployed parents, and the mothers (who are on the home front) are most likely to be the offenders.

One study also reports that in a deployed family, child neglect was almost four times greater than average, and the rate of physical abuse was twice as great (Hoge, 2005). This study reports that the primary offenders of child abuse are non-Hispanic white civilian females who are also suffering from secondary PTSD themselves. This often presents as emotional withdrawal, depression, increased anxiety, poor anger management, "living on the wild side", and even suicide (Hoge, 2005). From some of the interactions that I have had with military wives and girlfriends, I've learned there is even an increase in alcohol abuse while their partners are deployed. This just adds more challenges to the situation that children face. Once again, when the soldiers return, this becomes a new, unexpected, and, more than likely, unwanted and undesirable behavioral means of coping with stress. It is just another stress fracture on the home front.

Studies and historical accounts show that the healthier the foundation of the relationship, the better everyone fares in a variety of circumstances. However, with the military mindset, which is essential to a warrior's ability to maintain control and discipline, military families are not always able to nourish these foundations. The time requirements that our military personnel face sometimes prevent quality family time even after they return from being down range. It seems to be a Catch-22. However, I do know some very healthy, happy military couples who have managed to beat the odds and make time for each other and their children. They are the ones who do the best in weathering these challenging times.

Other qualities serve to solidify strong relationships, including a tremendous sense of pride and honor families have for the sacrifice that is being made by their warrior. This seems to be coupled with a deep level of respect by warriors for their partners who kept the home front fires burning during these long and dangerous deployments.

The behavior of the children varies, of course, according to age and the severity of their emotional stress. For the younger ones, we may see more regressive behaviors, separation anxiety, bed wetting, thumb sucking, the need to consistently sleep with the home front parents, and fear of going to school and leaving their attachment figure. With older school-aged children, we may see poor socialization skills, fights, a decrease in grades, poor concentration, severe anxiety, or a decline in athletic performance. With older kids, we may see an increase in defiant behaviors, pulling away from the parents, isolation, and acting out, such as the gang behaviors that have been reported in this particular age group. These kids are more than likely looking for an affiliation and a way to replace their dad or mom through drugs, alcohol, promiscuity, breaking laws, and reckless driving, just to name a few.

The teachers must be informed so that they know which of their students have deployed parents, the number of deployments, the duration, who is at home, and what their family life is like. This is where educators must start discussing (without overstepping bounds) the quality of social connections and if the students have church family, grandparents and extended family. The educators must know the status of the deployment, for example, when it is taking place or when they are returning. The way in which the teachers speak of the war and the possible spin they may put on circumstances is also a very sensitive topic.

We want our children to feel proud of their parents' service to our country, and we do not want them to feel like they must hide or withdraw out of fear of rejection and ridicule from their social group or from adult mentors. I have heard reports of teachers who have made blatant comments about a student's parent serving in the military with little regard for the impact it has on the child's soul. This is cruel and unprofessional. Teachers must be stewards of our children; it is up to them to carry the burden and not to compound things by coloring the feelings of their students by commenting on their parent's service.

It is very important for educators to understand the signs and symptoms of this particular stress in the students they teach. The most important thing here is that teachers recognize the outward characteristics, the challenges, and the nuances in behaviors that may not have been present or evident prior to the deployment. Change in behavior, and attitudes are good predictors of stress in students. Educators must be aware in order to offer support and intervene on behalf of the children and to help mitigate some of the negative and painful opinions of ill-informed and immature peers.

Since September 11, 2001, many American children have been touched by multiple deployments. According to the Pentagon and military historians, as cited by Maria Gold of the *Washington Post*, of approximately 263,000 people deployed overseas, mostly in Iraq and Afghanistan, about 43 percent are parents. In today's wars, unlike those of the past, that cycle is repeated for many families. Of 808,000 parents deployed since September 11, 2001, according to Pentagon data, more than 212,000 have been away twice. About 103,000 have gone three or more times. According to the 2007 Office of Army Demographics report, for every active duty army soldier (518,000), there is nearly one child (493,484) (Gold, 2008).

Children with a parent at war are vulnerable to adjustment issues such as anxiety or depression. Homecomings can also be particularly difficult as well, when parents return with physical or emotional wounds. According to a study conducted by the RAND Corporation, of the 1.6 million soldiers who have served in Iraq and Afghanistan, approximately 300,000 have PTSD or depression, and up to 320,000 may have suffered a traumatic brain injury (Jaycox, 2008). Experts are saying that these are the major wounds of this war, often referring to them as "invisible wounds." These are issues that may change the way the child's deployed parents may respond to them initially. It is important for the caring adult at home to work diligently with their child in dealing with transitions such as these. There are hundreds of thousands of children who will be affected by these deployments over time.

In regular units (army, Marines, air force, and navy), life for military families has always been one of expecting Dad or Mom to leave and go off to other locations to serve their country. It is considered their "job", and these families remain relatively steadfast with these constant changes. Children grow up with this way of life, and little is unexpected as far as deployments go. The current multiple deployments in OIF and OEF, however, have caught most nonregular military (National Guard, Enlisted Reserves) families off guard, and they've had to strive to find meaning and make sense of the sudden changes.

Together the National Guard and Reserves comprise almost half of the military capability of the United States. In 2004, more than 500,000 children had one or both parents serving in the National Guard or Reserves. The vast majority of these children were school-aged or younger.

This section introduces the issues and support assistance for those children who find themselves now in a new classification: overnight they have become military families. The sudden realization of just that alone can shake an entire family to the core, so a low-gradient education is a must. I recommend and encourage parents to help their children understand the following information.

What Is Deployment?

Loosely, the dictionary term for the word *deploy* means to "move out, spread out, or make use of", so when a parent gets deployed, they are moving out to actively use the skills they have learned in the military. Deployment occurs when a service member is assigned a military duty away from home and the family cannot accompany them. The parent may be deployed individually or with a group. The deployment may require special preparations or training for the service member to undertake before they leave for this remote duty.

Where Will My Daddy or Mommy Go?

It is important for children to get a crash course in geography, social studies, and cultural interests. Discuss the cultural aspects of the countries to which the parent has been deployed, and show those locations on a globe. It is a good idea to begin this process before your loved one deploys because this is an activity that can carry over during the deployment and can become just another way to stay connected. Talking about deployments from various angles will help children better understand what is happening to them and their families. (You might even use this as an opportunity to hone their math skills by calculating the distance in miles from home to the war zone.)

How to Prepare Children for Deployment

Children will have understandable fears for the safety of parents sent overseas. Therefore, it is important for you, the parent or family member, to know what to expect in children while their loved one is deployed. You can prepare the child first and foremost by educating yourself on spotting and dealing with their potential reactions to the new experience. It is crucial to provide opportunities for children to discuss their concerns and help them separate real from imagined fears. It is also important to limit exposure to media coverage of violence.

Parents and relatives at home can help by letting children honestly express their feelings and concerns. Frequent telephone calls, letters and/or e-mail are essential in helping children feel connected to, and loved by, absent parents. Because repeated scenes of destruction of lives and property are featured in the daily news media, they may understand that "enemies of the United States" can harm their loved one. Adults need to help children feel encouraged and safe at a time when the world seems to be a more dangerous place. As much as possible, we need to carry their share of the worry and pain that war causes. It is our duty as responsible adults.

I was once standing in an art display of very graphic Vietnam War scenes when a young mother came through leading a small boy of perhaps four years old. She was curious and wanted to take in what she could without spending a lot of time exposing her son to the impacting scenes. As she hastily dragged the boy along, he suddenly pointed at one of the paintings and asked, "Momma, what is that?" What she said next struck me as most profound. She wisely answered him, "Someday you'll know, but for now, I'll carry that load so you won't have to." She hurriedly exited the display and went about being a protective mom.

Emotional Responses

Emotional responses vary in nature and severity from child to child. Nonetheless, there are some similarities in how children feel when their lives are impacted by war or the threat of war.

- *Fear:* Fear may be the predominant reaction, especially fear for the safety of those in the military. When children hear rumors at school and pick up bits of information from television, their imaginations may run wild. They may think the worst, however unrealistic it may be.

- *Loss of control:* Military actions are something over which children—and most adults—have no control. This lack of control can be overwhelming and confusing. Children may grasp at any control that they have, including refusing to cooperate, to go to school, to part with favorite toys, or to leave your side.

- *Anger:* Anger is a common reaction and, due to its familiarity, may often be a substitute for expressing sadness or loss. Unfortunately, anger is often expressed at those to whom children are closest. Children may direct anger toward classmates and neighbors because they cannot express their anger toward those responsible for their parents being sent to war. Some children may show unexpected anger toward parents who are at home or those in the military, even to the extent that they do not want to write letters or draw pictures or send gifts. (This could be the child's way of developing their own "perimeter wire.")

+ **Loss of stability:** War or military deployment interrupts routines. It is unsettling. Children can feel insecure when their usual schedules and activities are disrupted, which increases their level of stress and need for reassurance. Even the adults are dealing with their own instability, and children are easily influenced by their environment. It is important to use good judgment in your daily behavior.

+ **Isolation:** Children who have a family member in the military, but who do not live near a military base, may feel more isolated. Children of reserve members called to active duty may not know others in the same situation. Such children may feel resentment and sadness toward friends whose families are intact (not deployed). They may strike out at signs of normalcy around them. Another group of children who may feel isolated are dependents of military families who have accompanied a remaining parent back to a hometown or who are staying with relatives while both parents are gone. Not only do these children experience separation from their parents, but they also experience the loss of familiar faces and surroundings.

+ **Confusion:** This can occur on two levels. First, children may feel confused about the concept of war and what further dangers might arise. Second, chil-

dren may have trouble understanding the difference between violence as entertainment and the real
events taking place on the news. Today's children
live in the world of *Armageddon, Independence Day,
Air Force One,* and cartoon superheroes. Some of
the modern media violence is unnervingly real.
Youngsters may have difficulty separating reality
from fantasy—cartoon heroes and villains from the
government soldiers and real terrorists. Separating
the realities of war from media fantasy does require
adult help.

What Parents Can Do

Everyone, including adults, feels stressed during times
of crisis and uncertainty. If your children seem to need help
beyond what is normally available at home or school, seek
mental health services in your community. Psychologists,
counselors, and social workers can identify appropriate services and help with the referral process. For most children,
adults can provide helpful support by the following actions:

Acknowledge children's feelings:

- Knowing what to say is often difficult. When no
  other words come to mind, a hug, a kiss, and saying
  "this is really hard for you/us" will help; but giving
  them an avenue of positive redirection by engaging
  them in a stimulating activity will do wonders.
- Try to recognize the feelings underlying children's
  actions and put them into words. Say something
  like, "I can see you have feelings about this. Tell me

more about them." Be careful not tell your children how *they* are feeling; instead let them tell you. A very good technique to express emotion is through art, music, dance, and acting. Invite the child to use these methods to physically demonstrate their feelings. (Younger children may find that using these alternative modes of communication are easier ways to express themselves.)

- Sometimes children may voice concern about what will happen to them if a parent does not return. If this occurs, offer something like this: "You will be well taken care of. You won't be alone. What would this look like to you if this happened? Let me tell you our plan and we can work together." If your child is mature enough, be sure to involve them in the dialogue, so they feel they are adding something constructive to the plan. Provide them with phone numbers of those whom you entrust them to; this will serve to provide an added sense of security for them. I did this with my daughter when she was in school and I was doing my graduate work, which took me away for long hours. She always knew who was on the list, and what she was to do if anything happened to me.

- At times when your children are most upset, do not deny the seriousness of the situation. Saying to children, "don't cry; everything will be okay," does not reflect how the child feels and does not make them feel better. You are essentially letting them know it is not okay to have feelings and emotions, and this is clearly a counterproductive message. Nevertheless, do not forget to express hope and faith that things will be okay, remembering to be truthful with what is appropriate for the age and situation. Determine whether or not your own fears are being projected onto your child. It is not appropriate for your child to carry your burden as well as their own.

- Older children, in particular, may require help clarifying what they believe about war and the role of the United States in the current conflict. They may ask some very poignant questions that you need to be prepared to address, such as, "will (my parent) kill someone?" and "Are we killing innocent people in other countries?" These issues may need to be discussed, so be prepared in advance. It may be a time to speak to a clergyperson and discuss the morality of war. Perhaps it is also good to remind the children that we hope our military can do enough to stop the war and help bring peace in other countries.
- Always be honest with children. Share your fears and concerns with discretion, at the same time reassuring them that responsible adults are in charge and they need not worry.
- If participation in a faith community is part of your family life, talk to your faith leader about how to help your child think about the concepts of death and killing in age-appropriate terms. This can be very important to calming your own fears, as well as those of your children. Talking to your clergy with or without your child is a great intervention because this does not signify trouble; this is a person of faith who can add a deeper level of understanding when attempting to make sense of these painful issues.
- Maintain normal routines and schedules to provide a sense of stability and security within the family, school and your community. Do not be afraid of calling in reinforcements for additional support for yourself and your child.

- Before your warrior comes home, start transitioning your child back to their own sleeping area rather than sharing your bed. Many of you have probably shared the family bed with your child, but this is a great risk for all concerned when your service member returns. Having a child in your bed can certainly be a very difficult or perhaps an impossible situation as your warrior needs to feel safe and know the child is safe also. But quality sleep is a must for all family members, and this cannot happen if you and your warrior sleep on eggshells. This is a critical point; I have talked to many who have been very uncomfortable with a child in bed, as nightmares sometimes take over the warrior, resulting in a very serious consequence.

Help children maintain a sense of control by taking some action and giving back.

- Send letters, cookies, or magazines to those in the military.
- Help older children find a family who has a parent on active duty; arrange some volunteer babysitting times for that family or offer to provide meals occasionally. These types of activities and support are vital for feeling a sense of purpose. As a community, you can all participate and serve by providing healthy and productive expressions of compassion.

If a family member is away, make plans for some special activities.

◆ Gatherings with other families who have a loved one on active duty can help provide support for you as well as for your children. This is a great way to build strong alliances with your military community.

◆ Special parent-and-child times can provide an extra sense of security which clearly adds to the ease of the transition. This also applies when your warrior returns because your child may need to get to know their deployed parent again after these long separations. Let your child know that you will set aside a particular half hour each day to play. Make the time as pleasant and child-centered as possible. Remember to return phone calls, emails and text messages later and make your child the real focus of that special time.

◆ Organize a consistent pattern that helps the child develop positive expectations, such as regular mealtimes. Morning and bedtime rituals (bathing, prayer, reading stories, etc.) can also provide a wonderful sense of peace and security for both parent and child. Rituals are routines that signal an event is about to occur; these will convey to you and your child when it is time to gear down or whichever activity is involved. Speaking of routine, here is one that was shared with me by a soldier. At the end of the day, he and his family would sit down for their meal, and during this time they would go around the table and tell something that was "bad" during their day, but always end the process with what was "good". I thought this ritual was wonderful because it offers a structured and safe venue for all family members to express their feelings, whatever they may be. This fosters cohesion and good, clear communication skills.

- Involve children in planning how to cope. Control and ownership are fostered when children help to plan strategies for dealing with a situation. Children often have practical and creative ideas for coping. Be open and willing to adjust your life accordingly. Be flexible without losing a sense of control. Most importantly, have fun and be sure to incorporate joy into your daily routine.

Expect and respond to changes in behavior.

- All children will likely display some signs of stress. Some immature, aggressive, oppositional, regressive, withdrawn, and isolative behaviors are reactions to the uncertainty of their situation. We advise that you seek professional help if these behaviors continue and are disruptive to you and your child. Just by having an objective third party to intervene can make a big difference in the well-being of your child's mental health and yours as well.
- Even though there has been a significant shift in the family structure, it is important to maintain consistent expectations for behavior. Be sure children understand that the same rules apply that were in place prior to the change or deployment. Do your best to maintain consistency.
- It is important that the roles in the family remain intact. For example, you are the parent and they are the children. You do not want to undermine this

principle by imposing false authority upon a child. For example, one of the most damaging expectations (or "assignments") is to say, "your dad has gone to war, so now you're the man of the house." I have even heard of servicemen who leave and say, "you are the man of the house, son." This wreaks havoc with the parent at home and the other children. It does not work. It confuses the child, who may now see this status as an added obligation and burden to uphold. On the other hand, it may also give them power to impose their rules upon the family system.

- Some children whose parents are on active duty may have difficulty at bedtime. Maintain a regular bedtime routine. Be flexible about night lights, siblings sharing a room, bedtime stories, sleeping with special toys, and sitting with your child as they fall asleep. Doing so typically does not create lifelong bad habits. Rather, these are comforting means to provide reassurance to a child.

Extra support, consistency, empathy and patience will help children return to routines and their more usual behavior patterns. If children show extreme reactions (aggression, withdrawal, sleeping problems, etc.), consult with a mental health professional regarding the symptoms of severe stress and the possible need for treatment. Do not wait—get in there and do a preemptive strike. This will serve you well and may ward off further and larger issues down the road.

Keep adult issues from overwhelming children.

- Do not let your children focus too much of their time and energy on the fact they have a loved one at war. If children are choosing to watch the news for hours each evening, find other activities for them. You may also need to watch the news less intensely yourself and spend more time in alternative family activities.
- Know the facts about developments in the war. Be prepared to answer your children's questions factually, and take time to think about how you want to frame events and your reactions to them. Take the high road—do not compound their negative feelings and fears with your own!
- Do not let financial strains be a major concern for your children. For National Guard or Reserve families, going from a civilian job to active duty in the military may cut family income. Children are not capable of dealing with this issue on an ongoing basis. Telling a child that you need to be more careful with spending is appropriate, but be cautious about placing major burdens on them. If they are older, once again include them in some of the planning that pertains to their spending.
- And finally... self-care. Take time for yourself and try to deal with your own reactions to the situation as fully as possible. This, too, will enhance your child's well-being. It is very important that you do what you can to build strong support systems, participate in stress-reducing activities, maintain a good diet and exercise program, set goals, rest, and spend reflective time in prayer or meditation. These are just

some quick suggestions, but you get the picture. You must take care of yourself, because you set the tone of the household, and when your warrior returns from deployment, you must be as intact as possible, so the homecoming will go as smoothly as possible.

Chapter Eight

Dual Deployments

...everywhere they stopped there were huge crowds gathered to cheer them on.
— Gary Paulsen, *Soldier's Heart*

What happens when both parents are enlisted in the military and both are deployed at the same time? This is a unique situation with its own set of issues for the entire family.

There are no rules preventing both a child's mother and father from heading off to war during the same period of time. So when orders come that land each of them in a combat zone, there are few options to consider. There is no military policy or federal law allowing any of the branches of service to refrain from sending a set of parents into a combat zone at the same time, and sadly enough, efforts to legislate change have fallen short.

So, what are some ways that families can weather this particular storm created by war? First, and probably most importantly, when both parents get deployed at the same time, it becomes an ultra-family event. Both sides of the family need to be prepared to meet the needs of any child in the couple's immediate family and to come together as a team to make sure that the home front remains intact. The second most important element is for dual-deployed families to tap into the support provided by family readiness groups that are active for their units. Since OIF and OEF were launched, the Family Readiness Groups (FRGs) have increased their visibility and consist of caring people who share a common experience of having a family member deployed. FRGs are a good arm of deployed military units; they specialize in keeping families informed, and they stay on top of what resources are available to them. These organizations have come a long way in their mission for families, and their functions are a good lifeline to have available. FRGs also sort out rumors that may be circulating. To know what is really true about an issue down range, ask your FRG leader; this will certainly set the record straight and help you to deal with excess anxiety.

Family Care Plan (FCP)

The importance of readiness and staying on top of your enlistment or military career cannot be overemphasized. One of the most important considerations of family readiness is to ensure that your family is taken care of during times of mobilization and deployment—especially during dual deployments. A Family Care Plan (FCP) is a must for every military family.

An FCP should be developed whether or not you expect to be deployed; in fact, many units will require that you develop a formal Family Care Plan. Taking care of these concerns beforehand will help you and your family be prepared for any period of separation.

When you do prepare your plan, be sure to address the following issues (please note this is not an exhaustive list, so be sure to check with your command to ensure that *all* your affairs are in order):

- Assign a guardian for your family in a special power of attorney (POA) and make sure that the guardian understands his or her responsibilities.
- Designate who will take care of your children if something were to happen to both of you.
- Make arrangements for animals and their care in your absence.
- Obtain ID and commissary cards and register in DEERS (Defense Enrollment Eligibility Reporting System, is a computerized database of military sponsors, families and others worldwide who are entitled under the law to TRICARE benefits), and check to make sure all ID cards are current and up-to-date.
- Sign up for Service Members Group Life Insurance, or a similar group life insurance, and update all beneficiary information.
- Arrange for housing, food, transportation, and emergency needs.
- Inform your family members or any caretakers about your financial matters.
- Arrange for any guardians to have access to necessary funds.
- Arrange for child care, education and medical care.
- Prepare a will and designate a guardian in the will.
- Arrange for necessary travel and an escort to transfer family members to their guardian.
- Discuss your plans with any older children.
- Stay current with documentation and requirements.

PART THREE

CHAPTER NINE

Positive Steps in Coming Home

He had forgotten none of what had happened. He knew it would come again. It had to come again because they were here. You did not have an army without a battle.
— Gary Paulsen, *Soldier's Heart*

In my work, I always do my best to help our troops and families. I always try to remind my readers and listeners of the impact and core issues of their military service and deployments. There are many hurdles surrounding multiple deployments. I have taken this information from my workbook course entitled *Once a Warrior: Wired for Life, An Interactive Workbook*. This is only a quick glimpse into the subject, and I encourage you to make the effort to do the entire course as soon as possible. However, if you and your partner can sit down and work through the following steps, I am positive that you will experience many wonderful benefits.

Taking the Steps

Those called to fight in a war are forever changed by what they see, what they do, and what they did *not* do. In many ways, those who come home will never be the same again. When one experiences the impacting effects of wartime service, profound changes sometimes take place. In the following steps, we will begin to discover what those changes are and find ways to work to rebuild lives and relationships.

Many veterans' partners and family members become perplexed that something has captured their loved one's soul. They feel as though the person who went off to war is not present enough in thought and spirit to devote themselves to their relationship. The service person is often distracted and caught up in vivid memories of an experience from the past. Until they sort through and gain some tools to deal with their issues, they will spend much of their time thinking about the past, rather than loving the ones who need them the most.

We will attempt to answer the questions, *where did my loved one go?* and *how do I get them back?* The following exercises will assist you in understanding and developing some tools to rebuild relationships.

#1. Reuniting with Loved Ones

Clearly, wartime deployments have a profound effect on the reentry process and with reacquainting with those we love. They can alter our ability to clearly see what is in front of us and may prevent us from objectively evaluating the reality of life's situations. In other words, one's image or belief about oneself and of others and their world have been transformed by the impacting events of being at war. When this happens the very foundation from which to understand one's world and meaning may be forever changed by one moment in time.

Expectations can easily be deceiving also. There is hardly anything worse than a failed expectation. Both the person waiting at home and the person waiting to come home have their own ideas as to what it will be like when they are reunited. Their dreams and hopes have been the fuel that has kept the anticipation of their reunification vibrant and alive. However, this anticipation can have some negative effects such as worry, fear and anxiety. Life has changed for both the person at home and for the one returning. Both parties may have developed different habits and patterns while being separated.

Here are some examples of these changes:

Time can be a major factor. The returning service person may demand much of their partner's time. The stay-at-home partner may have a problem with losing some "freedom", including not being able to spend as much time with the new friends they made during their partner's absence. They may even begin to miss the support network they were a part of while their loved one was away. Relationships that were formed independently in the absence of their partner could challenge the very foundation of their union.

The person at home more than likely may have developed a more independent view of life. Many tasks that were shared before the deployment, such as decision making about children, household duties, finances and social activities, may have now become the sole responsibilities of the stay-at-home person.

Perhaps it will be difficult to relinquish some of these duties. On the other hand, it may be that the person at home wants to "dump" everything back on the returning partner. However, the returnee may not be emotionally available to accept these demands.

At this point you may be asking yourself, *is the war experience going to block or hinder our intimate activities?* In order to answer this question, it is best to understand some mechanics regarding this aspect of relationships after war.

It is not unusual for people to have a startle response when caught by surprise. People who have had military training or have been in a military conflict may be quite vulnerable to sudden and unexpected turmoil or noise. A startle response is an involuntary reaction to a stimulus, that causes a person to retreat or attack without conscious thought. It has been shown throughout the centuries that war veterans have reacted with startle responses under stress even in civilian environments and this can lead to fear and rejection. It has even caused many relationships to end. For example, a veteran may be startled in his sleep and inadvertently attack the partner lying beside them; it may even be necessary for one partner to leave until a joint safety plan can be agreed upon.

If this is a possibility in your relationship, here are some important safety precautions that will help you cope.

A. Ensure that any weapons are secured in areas other than where the veteran lives and sleeps.

B. Choose and agree on separate sleeping quarters (private bedrooms) if sleeping in close proximity becomes problematic.

C. Do not argue or engage in upsetting dialogue before bedtime ("don't let the sun go down on your anger"). Instead, do everything you possibly can to resolve or put at bay any disagreement or heated discussions before retiring.

Intimacy

Last, but not least, is the topic of intimacy. Many couples wonder, *will our sexual relationship be different?* This may be a difficult area, but understanding the needs of each partner is important for a successful outcome. It can be challenging for a person to make the transition from war to peace, and intimacy with another person can be the benchmark of peace, on the far end of the spectrum from a war zone.

Often your reunion may not go as expected and the events you have been waiting for may not turn out as anticipated. Many couples are so caught up in the moment and wanting "it" to be perfect, that they try to encapsulate all their dreams into a short period of time. When this doesn't materialize like they planned, the impossibility becomes apparent and they realize they have set themselves up for a jolting disappointment.

Flexibility and creativity in the reunification are pivotal in restoring the level of intimacy that both partners desire. Here are some steps to help you create a smoother landing and begin to achieve normalcy in your relationship.

1. *Maintain a lower activity level.* Don't make plans to accomplish all your dreams in the first few days of your loved one's return. Unplug the phone and focus on each other.

2. Create the flavor of a getaway vacation. Keep it simple and easygoing.
3. If you have children, arrange for relatives or friends to keep them for a few days.
4. Capitalize on your loved one's favorites, including food, music, activities, entertainment, etc..
5. Pace yourself in your sexual connection. Find pleasure in rediscovering one another's personal desires. Sometimes females are fearful of how their partners will be with them, so just reassure them that they are safe and be sure to listen to their concerns.

Being deprived of intimacy for long months may present a variety of emotions. Uncertainty of one's partner's commitment and a sense of longing and anticipation are among the many apprehensions and hesitations that couples face upon reunification. Dreams and desires of the comfort and glow of intimacy can easily be shattered due to what each person experienced during their separation. Sometimes a warrior will return and not have the desire to make love because touch down range can be painful. Do not take this personally, but be open to these issues and don't rush it—it will be resolved over time.

An Inventory to Effectively Reuniting

The following are some activities to help you achieve positive results as you reunite with loved ones.

1. Openly discuss what routines you both have grown accustomed to, including the time spent with new friends and support groups during your absence from one another.

Communicate how you feel about not spending time with these people now that the reuniting process with your loved one has begun. With your partner, seek ways to find a balance that is satisfactory for both of you.

2. Make a list of those responsibilities and activities that you would like to retain/assume now that you are reunited. Once you are reunited, set aside quality time with your partner to discuss your feelings, concerns and considerations regarding these responsibilities and activities. Share this list with one another and discuss why you feel the way you do about these issues. Together, determine how positive results can be achieved.

Relating to Family

When a person leaves home to serve in the military, they are stepping out of one world into another. In most cases, they are thrust into a new environment overnight where they must readily adapt and learn to survive with a new set of rules in unfamiliar surroundings. A new soldier (sailor, airman or Marine) must strive to become a working participant in this new life. In the process, he or she usually develops a new persona and identity within this new "community". From day one of boot camp or basic training, they begin to change, and it is the drill cadre's primary job to facilitate this metamorphosis. Combining this with the tremendous personal danger and stress of wartime duty, a family member can easily see how their loved one will have changed during their time of service. This can be alarming for the unprepared family members. It is important to know that they probably will never get back their loved one in the same state of mind in which they left.

For example, one mother reports: "My son came home from months of desert fighting and hasn't unpacked his gear yet. He's still living out of his duffel bag in the middle of his old bedroom. He doesn't talk as often as he used to, and when he does talk, he's sharp with everyone in a way he never was before. He's different and living with him is a challenge."

This mother was not prepared to see her son come home this way. Understanding him and his behavior has become frustrating, and with no idea of how to cope or communicate with him, this situation could lead to years of estrangement.

"Advice" *Not* to Give

The following comments and misconceptions often do more harm than good. It is advisable to avoid them.

1.   Avoid telling a person who has gone through a stressful experience, "I understand where you're coming from", or "I know how you feel". If you have not experienced it yourself, the falsehood could alienate your relationship.

2.   Avoid telling a person that he or she needs to "just forget about it; it will go away with time", or "get over it!" because PTSD symptoms, if left alone, may worsen. Not talking about or not sorting through the issues does more harm than good. If the person will not or cannot talk to you about the issues, help them locate an experienced therapist. A veterans' support group can also be a likely choice if the service person is comfortable talking about his or her experiences in a group setting.

3.   Avoid unwarranted labeling of people who suffer from PTSD by telling them they have a "mental illness". Remember that most people subjected to the emotionally negative impact of war will never be the same again. The

experts say that PTSD is a normal response to an abnormal set of circumstances. The individual is reacting to life through the impressions of something that has taken them outside the range of normal human experience.

Steps for Relating with Family Members:

1. It is important to recognize and become familiar with the different aspects of how the service person has changed. Write out any observations about the changes you observe both in yourself and your loved one. Expand this list as you observe or experience the changes over a period of time, ensuring that these changes pertain to the context of your relationship. (This can be done both by the family member at home and by the returning service member.)

2. Indicate to the returning service person, because you love them and want to reconnect, that you place tremendous value on communicating about what has changed in their lives. Offer to make yourself available to listen to them talk about any of the issues and changes that they are willing to discuss.

3. Without forcing any issues or invading space and privacy, open up a dialogue on what in your lives has changed. Discuss with each other the changes that have occurred.

Steps in Readjusting to the Workplace (for returning warriors)

Warriors coming home are impacted in ways that make it difficult to adjust and reintegrate back into the workplace. These difficulties manifest themselves in a variety of ways. It is common for them to find it difficult to be around strangers and they may have problems with authority figures. Also, they may have a low tolerance for frustration.

Because most jobs require contact with other people (with at least a moderate degree of socialization) and contain hierarchies of employees, veterans are easily reminded of many negative aspects of military life. Incompetent chains of command are one common pet peeve. Too many times, the warrior may have witnessed inept combat leadership making poor decisions resulting in life-threatening scenarios and people being needlessly wounded or killed. The veteran may easily bring this deadly reminder into a "normal" workplace. They may find themselves rebuffing directions or "orders" from a superior who has not proven to be a good decision maker. Obviously, this is not conducive to job security. A work relationship like this can end in many negative ways, usually resulting in the veteran moving from job to job until finally they give up and remain unemployed. It is not uncommon to find veterans who have had dozens of jobs since returning from war. And not being able to achieve on such a viable level can negatively affect one's self-esteem.

The inability to maintain relationships on the job has many additional negative consequences and can create stress for the family as well. Financial security is of paramount importance in sustaining stable relationships. This stability is challenged when the veteran cannot maintain employment due to war wounds and/or stress.

The following are activities that may help you develop and maintain a satisfactory and rewarding work attitude.

Steps for Finding Satisfaction in the Workplace

1. Ask yourself the following questions:
   - Can I do this work without being reminded of or aroused by past memories of wartime or stress-filled experiences?
   - Am I more productive working in a protected environment (in the proximity of people I know and trust) rather than in an open environment where there are many people with whom I am unfamiliar?
   - Do I easily lose my concentration while working with other people? Am I easily distracted in the vicinity of random activity that I cannot control?
   - Can I multitask with minimal stress?

2. After drawing your conclusions from the points above, assess your ability to work successfully. Write down the type of work you enjoy doing and the conditions under which you would work the most effectively.

3. Determine which of the following is more important: (a) income level; (b) job satisfaction, or (c) work schedule (more hours or less hours worked). Ideally it would be best if all these factors were equally balanced and working in unison.

4. With your answer to Question 3 in mind, evaluate whether or not your military experiences are dictating the work you can do and how well you perform on the job. Ask yourself, *do I work or keep busy to avoid facing unresolved issues from my past?*

5. With the knowledge gained from the previous questions, chart out a course of action to seek, gain and maintain employment that will satisfy you and meet your emotional needs. (Consulting with a career advisor may be helpful in obtaining clarity in this area.)

Steps in Finding Meaning and Purpose from Your Experiences (for returning warriors)

During a war, little thought is given to what life will be like when it is over. However, we have seen what can happen if returning troops are not respected or if their duty assignments were misunderstood by society. Being left to their own devices to sort through these experiences has proven to be detrimental, and a sense of meaning and purpose for what has been experienced can be altered or lost.

It is a sad reality, but the military can ill-afford to prepare soldiers for the after effects of combat. If soldiers were told beforehand that their lives would be forever altered by what they saw, felt and did in combat, their perspective on the job at hand would be severely skewed. A young person cannot be promised anger, nightmares, anxiety attacks, hypervigilance, numbed feelings, alienation, guilt and the vast array of other debilitating after effects of war and still be expected to stay motivated to serve his or her country. Warriors cannot lose sight of the mission by focusing on the aftereffects of war.

Most warriors are not prepared for what is in store for them when they return home; they only have a feeling inside that their lives will surely be different now that "it" is over. Discovering meaning and purpose in what they have lived through is very important.

Steps in Finding Meaning and Purpose After Returning from War

1. Explain the details of your military responsibilities while serving.

2. Write down what you had hoped to gain from your military enlistment.

+   How was this different from what you expected?

+   How was it the same?

3. Now take a moment and thoroughly examine the following points (write down your responses and discuss them with your partner):

+   What life lessons have you learned as a result of your military experience?

- How has your spiritual awareness been affected? (How do you see yourself spiritually now?)

- How have these experiences and realizations changed your view of the future?

- How will these decisions affect you and your loved ones?

Determining the Quality of Your Relationship

Looking at the aspects of a successful relationship involves examining vital areas of communication, love, intimacy and boundaries. Successful relationships feature mutual respect, trust, unconditional acceptance, and freedom from judgment.

Relationships are ever changing, and this hopefully indicates that growth is occurring. However, if one party changes and it creates a risk to the relationship or to the other party emotionally, mentally, physically or spiritually, then it is definitely time to assess the quality of the relationship.

In order to assess and examine your relationship, let's see how you perceive your connection with one another.

An Inventory to Determine Relationship Quality:

1.   From the following list, mark the qualities that most likely describe your partner. Veterans, use the letter *V* next to your choice about your partner's traits, and likewise, partners use a *P* to indicate how you perceive them. Secondly, veterans, circle the qualities you would like to see improved in your partner, and partners, underline those qualities you would like to see improved in your veteran.

Kind	Fun-loving
Passionate	Intolerant
Sexual	Accepting
Adventurous	Critical
Beautiful	Demanding
Courageous	Selfish
Tender	Self-centered
Loyal	Crude

Handsome	Anxious
Selfless	Angry
Strong	Youthful
Funny	Volatile
Genius	Disrespectful
Innocent	Bullying
Admirable	Nagging
Talented	Controlling
Generous	Inconsiderate
Adorable	Inhibited
Patient	Reclusive
Loving	Distant
Steadfast	Lazy
Committed	Depressed
Hardworking	Unpredictable
Honest	Unforgiving
Sensitive	Negative
Motivated	Pessimistic
Compassionate	Boring

2.   If your partner is completing this inventory along with you, please take a few moments to compare your results. Now you are on your way to reconnecting with your loved one. Remember, when sharing, use the phrase "I see you as_____." Keep it productive. Do not take it personally. Instead, take this exercise as an opportunity to reestablish a connection and know each other better.

3. *Expression of Wishes:* Indicate to each other any particular needs that have arisen during the period of absence. For example: "I had to be both mom and dad while you were away, and now I need you to resume your role." Discuss these needs and concerns in detail.

4. *Expression of Appreciation:* Validate the good changes you have seen in each other by using encouragement. For example: "I appreciate the sacrifice you have made for our country and how you have made the effort to readjust." The veteran could say, "I appreciate how you have shouldered the load in my absence, and I want you to know that this has increased my love for you." Write down and discuss other ways both of you can show appreciation for one another.

Improving the Quality of Relationships

A healthy relationship involves developing certain traits where commitment and dedication are at the helm. (There is a distinct difference between those two precepts.) We can easily add to this list: communication, a focus on reality, affinity, trust, honesty, perseverance, humor, physical touch, and quality time spent together. It is important for you to discover what qualities are the most important in order to rebuild your relationship and to connect with your loved one(s).

Along with these relationship traits, it has been determined that every human is born with basic needs: shelter, food, clothing and love. Our parents or other grown-ups meet most of these needs when we are young. However, for some, life is not so simple. These needs may not be consistently met, and as adults we are left unable to self-soothe or to feel whole as a person. As we mature and become more independent from our parents, we begin to seek others with whom we can experience mutual fulfillment of our emotional, spiritual and physical needs. An awareness of these basic needs prepares you to take the next step in this relationship exercise.

Steps to Improve the Quality of Your Relationships

1. *Affection* is defined as "love expressed."

How do you express love?

How would you like to have love expressed to you?

2. *Acceptance* is referred to as making it "okay" to be ourselves.

How do you see yourself? (Who do you think you are?)

How do you accept others? (What do you do to let others be themselves?)

3. *Attention* indicates that we are important and that we matter.

How does your partner recognize and acknowledge your importance?

In what ways do you communicate the importance of your partner?

4. *Affiliation* is defined as a sense of "belonging".

How does being connected in this relationship give you a sense of belonging?

5. *Approval* is a desire to be appreciated and supported for your abilities and personal qualities.

How do you demonstrate approval of your partner?

How do you recognize approval from your partner?

6. *Affirmations* are positive words and actions that reinforce and validate our goodness in this life.

In what ways do you appreciate being affirmed by your partner or loved ones?

What positive words and actions do you use to acknowledge your partner's goodness?

How do you reinforce and validate the goodness you see in others?

Now take a few moments to express at least three affirmations about yourself and someone close to you.

1.

2.

3.

A Trusting Relationship

A veteran once told me that if he did not distrust people, then he would have to trust them. He went on to say that he just could not trust others because he was not ready to deal with being betrayed again.

Trauma exposure clearly affects one's ability to discern or even desire a "normal" relationship. Relationships that were formed while serving in the military were based on the perspective and commitment that one would be *willing to lay down their life for another person.* It is all about trust and camaraderie.

Veterans have shared the deepest of human emotions: terror, vulnerability, hope, love and despair. They learned to bond based on these common emotions, and they formed connections that journey to the very depths of their souls. Consequently, the quality of these relationships is unique and is not usually replicated in subsequent relationships outside of the military. This is a major challenge in reconnecting with loved ones.

When loved ones sense their service member is putting up a perimeter or a boundary, it begins to feel like they are not being let in. Of course, this is difficult for the service person to explain. They often say, "you weren't there; you don't understand." It ultimately becomes a matter of trust, trust that the family and loved ones need to regain with their loved one. "So, how?" you may ask, "how can my warrior make the needed transition to trust in civilian life? How does one go about it?" Here are some ideas for you.

Work Together on the Following Commitments

Commitment requires a large degree of trust. In order to begin your journey in developing trust and commitment, accept and practice the following agreements:

- Agree to avoid hurting one another.

- Agree to acknowledge the validity of the other person's viewpoint.

- Agree to express empathy (understanding what it feels like to be in the other person's shoes).

- Agree not to hide your feelings from one another (be vulnerable with each other).

- Agree not to abandon each other in the face of the worst storms (be steadfast).

- Agree to work out conflicts with each other (find middle ground on issues).

- Agree to take responsibility for your actions and make an effort to change in order to strengthen the relationship.

- Agree to admit your own faults and wrongdoings. Be quick to ask for forgiveness when you fall short of expectations.

Steps for a Trusting Relationship

The person returning from deployment may have concerns about what to expect when they get home. Will they be able to discuss the experiences they had during deployment? (From experience, we have found that it is not realistic to think that loved ones will always have an interest or the capacity to hear what you have to say about your time away.) A common concern for returning troops is, "who will I talk to? Who will understand my experience and feelings?" If your partner will not attempt to understand or is not interested in discussing your concerns—or if you don't want to share these experiences with them—then this may create more distance in the relationship.

Here are some tools that may help in this matter:

1. Briefly describe a time in your relationship when you felt you could trust your partner the most.

2.   Recall a situation when you and your partner shared the same point of view. Now describe a time when you disagreed. Discuss with your partner how you both came to accept one another's point of view.

3.   Sharing the experiences of your military service can help develop empathy and increase the level of trust between you and your loved ones. However, to avoid frustration it is advisable that your loved ones are enthusiastic about wanting to hear what you have to share. Consider the areas of your military life that you are prepared to discuss. How can you help your civilian partner understand your feelings concerning a stressful event during your military service?

4.   Stressful experiences cause us to put on an "invisible emotional overcoat". This gives us the illusion that our secrets are protected and no one will ever find out what we really think, feel or regret.

How can you take off your emotional protective overcoat and reveal your true self to your partner? Write down what you discover and communicate these findings to your partner. Remember to pace yourself as feelings arise. Do it at a safe cadence as you go through this process.

5. A sense of abandonment is a serious issue for those who have served and lost friends in combat. List and discuss what you need from your partner in order to feel reassured about the strength, stability and permanence of your relationship.

(*A caveat:* Each of you has different kinds of relationships, and the information presented in this section could also allow single warriors to have better success. We all have relationships of many kinds—friends, parents, siblings and significant others. Take your time and start the process of dialogue when you are ready to engage. It may take some time. In the meantime, evaluate how your actions are affecting the relationships around you. Ask yourself, *is what I am doing turning toward the relationship or turning away from the relationship?* Keep in mind that using a great deal of self-control when you are "activated" (experiencing a trigger from your war experiences) is in your best interest. Watch your posturing, the volume of your voice, and the kind of words you use. You can easily come across as hostile or intimidating because this type of communication was vital and very useful in the war zone.

For those on the home front, be mindful of your contribution to these communication patterns. Do not run after your warrior, hit him or her, or physically attempt to restrain them as this can become a very volatile situation for both of you. Because domestic violence is common among returning warriors, this, coupled with alcohol and poor communication, can be extremely dangerous. Agree while in a calm state to have a plan in place if you get too upset during interactions with each other. What I mean by this is to take thirty minutes away from each other to calm down. Then you can return and restart the process of communication in a calm, constructive manner. This will serve you well in the long road of reconnecting with people in your life. If you find that you are not able to communicate about the topic at hand without getting angry it may be time to call in the reinforcements, such as a third party (i.e. battle buddy, therapist or chaplain).

CHAPTER TEN

A Transition Tool Kit

The training must work, he thought.
I'm doing all this without meaning to do it.
                    — Gary Paulsen, *Soldier's Heart*

The return to civilian life is a major transition. But with a good plan in place and some foresight, you can effectively control the process. This small section is intended to help you create a game plan for a successful transition back to civilian life.

Most people who have served say that military life is not easy, but many will also verify that leaving the military is not easy either. When you separate from the service, there are many decisions to be made and many procedures and forms to follow. If you are not prepared for this, it can be overwhelming. As time draws near to separation, you should schedule an appointment with a transition counselor. All military units are required by law (Public Law 101-510) to make these counselors available for service members. I recommend that you set up your separation counseling appointment at least 180 days prior to separation, but the law requires it be done at least 90 days before.

The Career Change

The task of changing careers is usually one of the first challenges you will encounter in the transitional process. Career transitioning from the military to civilian life is not that different from simply changing from one civilian job to another; they all seem to go through the same fundamental stages:

- Job search
- Job selection
- Job retention, success and support

Although "job search" is in the first position in this list, for you job selection" may be the first step to take. Many times it makes more sense to get an idea of what you would like to do and then begin the search for it. If you have an idea of what you would like to do and then zero in on a potential business or company and apply there, the process may seem to make more sense, especially when it comes to writing a résumé. A résumé that is *streamlined* for a particular company or skill not only makes you seem more qualified, but it helps the employer see how you are the right person to help them achieve their goals. You immediately present yourself as a team player. And with job selection, you do not have to take the first job that comes along. Take into account the type of work, the location, the salary and benefits, and how the opportunity will enhance your future career.

However, many employers do not like to hire the un-employed (as biased as that may be), so even if you do take the first job offer, you do not need to feel locked into it. A good solid move may be to look for a suitable job that can suffice for the time being and then move on to a better one as it becomes available. Consider this to be part of the process of advancement.

Once you have selected a career direction, the challenge of finding work begins. Tens of thousands of people all across the country are hired each year, and many of them are making career changes. Employee turnover opens up existing opportunities all the time, and thousands of entirely new jobs are created as the world advances and changes with the times. However, it is always wise to be alert and prepared for the challenges too; the job market is more competitive than ever. The best way to improve your odds is to seek the opportunities for which you are best prepared.

Also, network! Most jobs today are filled by referrals, not want ads. Develop and use your network of friends, colleagues and family members as starting points. Local personnel offices and community colleges are also a good source for networking for positions. Likewise, there are always many local, state and federal job-hunting seminars held each year that specialize in résumé writing and interviewing techniques. Attend job fairs and keep your eyes open for opportunities that pop up.

Continue to refine your game plan as you anticipate your separation from the service. One form (DD Form 2648) serves as a checklist to keep this pre-separation game plan in order. It can be downloaded easily from the web or obtained from your unit or installations transition offices (Command Career Counselor's Office or the Marine Unit Transition Counselor's Office).

Assess your job skills and interests. Determine how they fit into the job market. Visit *www.careers.org* to find helpful information about researching job and career opportunities. While this site may seem like an overload of information, it is still good to check it out. Just don't let it bog you down.

Prior to separation, continue to research specific job possibilities and stay abreast of job markets and economic conditions in the geographic area where you will be living.

Stress Related to Leaving the Military

Because you have been in the military for some time, it is to your advantage to understand the stress involved in separating from that lifestyle. You will need certain coping tools to meet the challenges brought on by that stress.

When you leave the military, one of the first challenges you will most likely encounter has to do with your identity. When you are on military duty, you have a rank and a service branch. If someone asks you who you are and what you do, you generally answer, "I'm a US Marine", or "I'm a sergeant in the army", or "I'm a petty officer in the US Navy." With those answers, everyone around you knows what you mean. However, when you leave the military, suddenly you find that you are only a civilian with the plain title of Jack, Sarah or Michael. This alone can cause some anxiety and perhaps even some confusion. For example, when a person completes the required studies to become an accountant, they may acquire the title of "CPA" (Certified Public Accountant), and it really does not need much more explaining than that. A person leaving the military, on the other hand, may work years to achieve a certain rank and job skills, but when they separate from the service they leave that rank and Military Occupational Specialty (MOS) behind—and with it a large portion of their identity.

This can be stressful, but remember that stress is not a sign of not being able to handle things. It is a real physical response that, if not addressed or if left unchecked, can lead to some undesirable consequences. Here are some important signs of stress overload to look out for:*

- Constant fatigue
- Headaches
- Trouble sleeping or sleeping too much
- Stomach problems
- Frequent colds or other illnesses
- Smoking or drinking more than usual
- Feeling nervous much of the time
- Being more irritable or angry than you want to be
- Wanting to be alone; avoiding other people

*If you are dealing with more than one of these symptoms, you may want to consider getting some professional assistance.

A transition of this magnitude is likely to become stressful for you and your family, but here are a few easy coping tools you can use to effectively deal with stress related to military separation:

- *Don't sit still:* This transition belongs to you and no one else. It is important to keep busy and be as productive as you can during this time.
- *Make you and your skills known:* Remember how important your skills are. Don't be modest about your accomplishments and training. It is the person who

141

is proactive that gets the jobs and succeeds on a mission. No one will come looking for you unless you make yourself known—so go out and "sell yourself"!

- *Be methodical in your transition:* Plan your transition and work at it as if it was a job to be done. However, don't burn yourself out by spending every waking moment at this "job". Take time for yourself and set a pace that is satisfactory for you. You, as an individual, and your family are the priority in this process. Get together often with them and have some fun. <u>Maintain balance in your personal life and career pursuits.</u>
- *Mindfulness:* Consider taking a mindfulness-based stress reduction program that is now offered by most VA hospitals. These programs are designed specifically for people who are experiencing the signs of stress in daily life and want to achieve more balance. The program also complements the medical management of illness, chronic pain, and stress-related disorders. Intensive training in mindfulness meditation, gentle movement such as yoga, qigong, and walking meditation, and group support are all important aspects of these programs. Mindfulness basically means being completely in touch with, and aware of, the present moment. The idea is to place oneself in a position to approach life experiences in non-judgmental ways. For example, a mindful approach to one's past (and present) experiences involve simply viewing "thoughts as thoughts" as opposed to evaluating certain thoughts as positive or negative. In other words, try to begin looking at the world from a more relaxed view, not as right or wrong. Mindfulness can have many benefits for people suffering from difficulties such as anxiety and depression.

Securing Important Documents

One of the first important documents to secure and keep safe is your DD Form 214. It is the lasting record (and verification) of your military service. Without a DD Form 214, no programs offered to veterans will be available to you. This form is one of the most critical forms the service will ever give you, and it is the key to participation in all the Department of Veterans Affairs (VA) programs and services on both a state and federal level. Keep your original DD Form 214 in a safe, fireproof location, and make certified photocopies that can be used for reference. Many veterans lose this form over the years, and it takes time to replace it. This is time that you may not have, so keep it in a safe place. Remember, time may be of the utmost importance in getting things done, especially during the transition period.

If you do lose the DD Form 214, here is how to order another:

Write to the National Personnel Records Center and request a new one. Include the following information in your request:

- ◆ Your full name
- ◆ Social security number
- ◆ Current phone number (don't forget the area code)
- ◆ Approximate dates of service (if you do not know exact dates)
- ◆ Place of discharge
- ◆ Return address
- ◆ Reason for the request (lost, etc.)

Send the request to:

National Personnel Records Center
Attention: (Your branch of service, i.e., Army, Marine Corps) Records
9700 Page Boulevard
St. Louis, MO 63132-5000
Phone inquiries at: (314) 538-4261

You should obtain other important service documents and secure them safely as well. Never give an original copy of these documents to anyone else. This includes service-issued licenses, certificates, performance ratings, security clearances and medical records. One last and very important document to mention here is the DD Form 2586: "Verification of Military Experience and Training". Be secure, and remember... be safe.

Caveat: Since we are talking about securing and maintaining important records, be sure to obtain your medical records, including examinations, diagnostic findings, and appointment notes. Also, if you have any emails, personal journals, or letters that you have written, please make copies of them and put them in a safe, secure location. In the future, you may need to refer to these important documents to verify an event that occurred while serving in the military or a medical issue that became more notable over the years. It is a good idea to maintain a personal journal for future reference as well. Some of the veterans whom I counsel can no longer remember some of the key players they served with and have no way of contacting them. So take time to get some basic contact information from those in your unit. Do not make the same mistake and lose contact.

All of this information can save you and those representing you a lot of time if ever you need verification for a rating decision for disability, social security, or other benefits.

One more note of advice: If you are returning to school or to the work force, register with your vet representative in these institutions. Let them know if you have been classified officially disabled. This will allow you to take advantage of particular benefits that you are entitled to in order to help with this transition. If you are not classified as officially disabled, please inform your school counselor or employer if you require assistance with various aspects of your education or job. You must be proactive in order to be successful and inform those around you if you need help. For example, if you are having difficulty with sleep, you may find it challenging to get to work on time, concentrate or deal with frustration. Informing your instructors or employers of issues such as these may help you maintain your course more successfully in the long run. Look for ways to calm yourself down, take a stress break, and reestablish yourself in the present time. This will go a long way in helping you persevere.

AUTHOR'S NOTE

A Summary of the Issues and Answers on the Home Front

Why do combat veterans struggle so much with their return to civilian life? One reason may be the issue of "rank". In the military, the troops don't make decisions as equals. You get an order and you follow it. You don't discuss your feelings. You don't hear the reasoning behind the order. You simply obey the one who outranks you.

The same is true if you are a leader. When you give an order, you don't expect to explain yourself or to have to listen to everyone's feelings about your order. You expect obedience. Military members often carry this hierarchy of rank over into their personal lives.

We've all heard of military commanders who try to parent their children as though they were in basic training. That kind of parenting doesn't work well with our children, and it is especially detrimental to interpersonal relationships. If you care about your partner, you must value their needs and wants, remembering that their viewpoints and insights are just as important as yours.

A relationship has nothing to do with rank. Relationships are formed by equals and involve putting effort into really getting to know one another. You both must put time and energy into exploring the differences between the two of you in order to understand your similarities, and vice versa.

Another way combat training may interfere with integrating back into civilian life and finding "middle ground" has to do with human biology. As we strive for the peaceful resolution of conflicts, it's important to know something about adrenaline, the "juice" that drives most of us from day to day. It also gets us into trouble in our relationships. It sometimes overrides our judgment and leads to behaviors and decisions that can be detrimental to our relationships.

How Adrenaline Works

Each of us was born with adrenal glands. Located on the top of each kidney, the adrenals are small glands that are stimulated by the autonomic nervous system. When we become upset or frightened, these glands secrete survival hormones, chemicals that pour into the bloodstream giving us new energy and strength to overcome perceived dangers. This sudden flow makes us stronger and more alert. It also protects us from blood loss, increases our lung capacity, focuses our vision, and directs blood flow away from unnecessary organs to the large muscles of the body. In other words, the adrenaline serves to hone in our natural instincts for survival.

These physical changes are commonly referred to as the "fight or flight" response. For example, it enables a frightened wife to lift the car off her injured husband or a terrified person to run long distances for help. With this system fully functioning, our physical capacity to do extraordinary things borders on the supernatural.

While this system helps keep us alive in the face of extraordinary danger, it does have one major flaw. The human brain cannot differentiate between a real threat and an imagined one! The brain doesn't notice (or care) if it has encountered something real or a memory that has been triggered from something in our immediate surroundings. Determined to keep us safe, it simply sends out the signal to react. This is reinforced by military training. The adrenaline flows, and sometimes we may even function with an "out-of-body" response.

Adrenaline flowing from a "false need" can result in a precarious reaction. It can be notably dangerous to our own health as well as the health of those nearest to us. Not only does it add stress to normal body organs, like the heart and circulatory system, but the constant presence of adrenaline can become quite addictive as well. Many trauma survivors seek the next adrenaline "rush" and do not feel complete without routinely having this experience. Thrill-seeking behavior after surviving something that has "turned on" our system is a common response. Life can be pretty boring without this feeling of vitality, but at the same time it can result in negative consequences if it interferes with our ability or desire to devote time to a relationship.

In relationships, the adrenaline response almost always works against us. Once the process begins, adrenaline is nearly impossible to control—especially after months of combat, where survival depended on adrenaline for prolonged periods of time. This is an automatic response pattern, so it is important to be aware of the messages your body receives in order to head the reaction off at the pass.

In human relationships, the adrenaline cycle can send us down two equally destructive pathways. First, you have heard about the combat veteran who suddenly dives for cover when he (or she) hears a car backfire or fireworks explode. The noise signals danger; the brain, unable to differentiate between a real or imagined threat, initiates the adrenaline cycle. An old imprinted message says, *move into action to survive!* The person does not have time for conscious thought; the familiar response takes over just like it did in combat, but most of the time this response is inappropriate for the situation on the home front.

The trigger can be a smell, sound or any combination of other sensory perceptions that may be associated with a past injury or threat. When these sudden triggers occur, a veteran may suffer tremendous emotional upset. The pain, fear, helplessness and confusion of horrific wartime experiences might surface immediately, not to mention the disappointment or embarrassment that may be part of the package.

When this cycle plays out in the presence of those close to the veteran, they, too, become affected by these behaviors. I have had many spouses vent their frustration to me about how little they understand what is happening to their loved one. They feel helpless to change situations as they arise. In order to obtain a better understanding of the effects of combat trauma, education is vital. If family members do not take the time to learn about this adrenaline cycle, resentments may be formed and they themselves may begin to move away from the relationship.

Not only is education important, but the social support among others who have similar experiences can do much for emotional stability. One very bright young wife recognized the need for support, and she had a therapist (me) in place when her husband returned from Iraq. It was very rewarding to help them both gain insights into his behaviors, which could have caused a great deal of distress in their relationship had she not been as proactive.

Children are certainly affected by the process of deployment. Sometimes both parents are deployed at the same time and this creates unique challenges for children, extended family members, friends and the troops who are deployed. Many behaviors can indicate stress symptoms in children; however, this varies according to age. Regressive behaviors could occur, such as bed wetting, thumb sucking, feelings of insecurity, being more needy for attention, poor sleep patterns, and fear of being left alone. Older children may show signs of anxiety or depression in other ways. They may sleep longer, use drugs or alcohol, be less cooperative at home, or isolate themselves from others. These are just some examples, but it is clearly not an exhaustive list of possibilities.

Parents or other adults should help children understand their emotions, provide support, and not burden them with issues best carried by adults. In order to help them discern the difference between reality and fantasy, use language that does not alarm them and monitor the programs they watch on television, including the computer games they play.

Teachers are also a good first line of defense. They are in a position to observe and address subtle changes in their students' behavior, school performance, and peer interactions. It is vital for parents to alert the teacher of their concerns about their children and the circumstances that could affect them.

Family members, as well as those returning from deployment, need to receive emotional support from those experts who truly understand the adjustment issues associated with deployments and trauma reactions.

Many of the VA hospitals now have deployment clinics that are doing their best to streamline the red tape and get the service member registered and in the system. Veterans are entitled to two years of care for medical issues through the VA federal system, and it is critical that they get established as soon as possible to assure care.

There are also options available for those who are fearful of going into the VA system: Military One Source is good because they can refer the service person to a mental health provider in the community and off base. There are also programs available in some states—such as Washington, where I am a PTSD Mental Health Contractor (for more information, visit *www.dva.wa.gov.com*)—that provides free mental health care to active duty servicemen and women, veterans and their families.

Back to the topic of adrenaline, one phenomenon that occurs frequently is episodes of "flight." These can catch any unsuspecting veteran or heavily traumatized person off guard. Out of a sense of protection for loved ones, the survivor may withdraw, isolate or dissociate. The resulting distance is a breeding ground for the erosion of healthy relationships.

The second pathway is equally as destructive. The flowing adrenaline produces a type of high that was perfectly acceptable in the war zone. That high, commonly known as an adrenaline rush, can also be described as *rage*. However, while acting out with rage during combat may be necessary, it can become an all-too-familiar pattern in the civilian world. Sadly, these behaviors or violent responses in civilian environs (in times of danger or perceived danger) have resulted in the incarceration of many veterans, as well as destroyed lives.

During the years I've spent working with combat veterans and their families, I have found that the more trauma survivors learn about the dynamics of their experience, the easier it is for them to make positive changes. So, in relationships, we need to go back to square one and work forward from there.

Learning the techniques of reaching a middle ground and applying these techniques to situations in life is critical to fending off many negative behaviors and reactions. Searching for, finding and isolating personal triggers (along with "perimeter wires" that do not allow others to get close) is paramount to achieving peace in our lives.

A Timeless Relationship

"I'm not supposed to see this, God. No person is supposed to see this. How can You let this happen?"
— Gary Paulsen, *Soldier's Heart*

In this book we have been on a journey that so intricately weaves through our souls that I cannot avoid the mention of how valuable a spiritual connection can be. In light of this, I want to share a thought for you to consider. I offer this to you solely as a word of encouragement and not as an attempt in any way at religious persuasion. However, I have found that to have faith in something larger than ourselves can be powerful and comforting, especially following highly stressful situations in life.

There is much to be said for setting goals, but the most powerful goal is inner peace and calm in the midst of a storm. Such peace will help you cope with many situations that arise. Whenever you keep the big picture in mind, whatever that may be for you, it keeps things in perspective.

With this peace in mind, I suggest one of the most important relationships to any of us is the one we have with our spiritual belief system. Don't neglect it, as this can buffer the pain and help you put meaning into a void where before there may have been only questions and uncertainty.

I remind warriors that we as humans cannot make sense of many of the things that happen in life, particularly in war. This is why it is so important to rise above the pain and suffering and create an internal personal sanctuary. This is a place of reverence where we can connect with higher ground in order to find peace and hope.

I am sure you have heard the old adage, "there are no atheists in a foxhole". It is true that when we are pushed beyond our emotional limits, a common response is to reach out in prayer. It is my personal prayer that whatever choice you make in your spiritual journey, let it be the best one you've ever made.

Bridget C. Cantrell, Ph.D.

RECOMMENDATIONS

The following are books that I recommend for warriors, partners, loved ones, and friends. For each book, I have listed contact information for those interested in placing an order.

Cantrell, Bridget C. & Dean, Chuck, *Down Range: To Iraq and Back*
www.heartstowardhome.com (360) 714-1525, Ext. 2

Cantrell, Bridget C. & Dean, Chuck, *Once a Warrior: Wired for Life*
www.heartstowardhome.com (360) 714-1525, Ext. 2

Dean, Chuck, & Nordberg, Bette, *When the War Is Over: A New One Begins*
www.pmim.org 1-989-584-6201

Dean, Chuck, *'Nam Vet: Making Peace with Your Past*
www.pmim.org 1-989-584-6201

Kay, Ellie, *Heroes at Home: Help and Hope for America's Military Families*
www.bethanyhouse.com

Martin, Hilary, *Solo Ops: A Survival Guide for Military Wives*
orders@xlibris.com

Chapman, Gary, *Five Languages of Love*
Northfield Publishing www.amazon.com

Pavlicin, Karen, *Surviving Deployment: A Guide for Military Families*
www.amazon.com

Tick, Edward, *The War and the Soul*
Illinois: Quest Books

The New Warrior: Combat Stress and Wellness Perspectives for Veterans and Their Families. The Department of Veterans Affairs, 27 min.. Quicktime and Windows Media format, http://www.ncptsd.va.gov/ncmain/ncdocs/videos/emv_newwarr_vets.html?opm=
"The wars in Iraq and Afghanistan are the most sustained combat operations since the Vietnam War. These videos aim to help promote wellness in this returning group of veterans and to prevent chronic mental health issues resulting from combat and other war-zone stress. It is available both as a video for veterans, active duty service members and their families, as well as a version with provider perspectives."

BIBLIOGRAPHY

Gibbs, D. A., Martin, S. L., Kupper, L. L., & Johnson, R. E. (2007, August 1). Child Maltreatment in Enlisted Soldiers' Families During Combat-Related Deployments. *JAMA*, 298(5). 298:528-535.

Gold, M. (2008, July 17). Coping With Their Parents' War: Multiple Deployments Compound Strain for Children of Service Members. *Washington Post*, pp. A01.

Hoge, C. (2005, July 22). *Walter Reed Study Department of Defense Study. Stars and Stripes.*

Jaycox, L., & Tanielian, T. (2008, April 17). *One In Five Iraq and Afghanistan Veterans Suffer from PTSD or Major Depression.* Arlington: Rand Corporation.

Kanter, E. (2006, November 6). High Rate of PTSD in Returning Iraq War Veterans. *Medscape Medical News.*

Paulsen, G. (2000). *Soldier's Heart: Being the Story of the Enlistment and Due Service of the Boy Charley Goddard in the First Minnesota Volunteers.* New York: Dell Laurel-Leaf.

About the Author

Dr. Bridget C. Cantrell is a member of the American Psychological Association and Association of Traumatic Stress Specialists, and President/CEO of Hearts Toward Home International, a charitable nonprofit organization dedicated to the recovery and reintegration of trauma survivors. Her primary work encompasses therapeutic counseling for war veterans and their families.

With a Ph.D. in clinical psychology, Bridget is a licensed mental health counselor in the State of Washington and a nationally board-certified mental health counselor. She currently works as one of a small number of specially selected and trained Washington State Department of Veterans Affairs PTSD contractors. In 2008 and 2004, she was named Outstanding Female Non-Veteran for her service to veterans by the Washington State Governor's Veterans Affairs Advisory Committee and the Washington State Department of Veterans Affairs. In 2008, she was honored to receive the Erasing the Stigma Leadership Award from the Didi Hirsch Mental Health Center in Los Angeles, California. In 2008, her organization, Hearts Toward Home International, was selected as 2008 Best of Bellingham in the Non-Profit Charitable category by the US Local Business Association (USLBA).

Presently, she provides mental health services to troops from all branches of the military, including active duty, reservists, the guard, and their families. This work focuses on providing effective tools for military personnel to readjust after experiencing the impact of combat exposure, trauma, family deployment stress, and many other readjustment issues after service in a war zone. She is regularly invited to teach and present to mental health providers, civilian caregivers, and military units around the world.

Dr. Cantrell travels extensively, teaching and lecturing to military personnel and their loved ones regarding the different aspects and issues of trauma and reintegration after experiencing war. She works throughout the European and Pacific duty assignments and is headquartered in Bellingham, Washington.

Please feel free to contact the author about any part of this book or with questions you may have regarding the many phases of deployment or reintegration.

**To order additional copies and bulk quantity orders
or to arrange a workshop, please contact:**

Hearts Toward Home International
(an IRS Approved 501 (c) (3) Public Charity)
1050 Larrabee Avenue
Suite 104, PMB 714
Bellingham, Washington 98225-7367
(360) 714-1525 (Extension #2)
www.heartstowardhome.com